Lincoln and Leadership

The North's Civil War
Paul A. Cimbala, series editor

Lincoln and Leadership

Military, Political, and Religious Decision Making

Edited by
Randall M. Miller

FORDHAM UNIVERSITY PRESS
NEW YORK 2012

Copyright © 2012 Fordham University Press

All rights reserved. No part of this publication may be reproduced, stored in a retrieval system, or transmitted in any form or by any means—electronic, mechanical, photocopy, recording, or any other—except for brief quotations in printed reviews, without the prior permission of the publisher.

Fordham University Press has no responsibility for the persistence or accuracy of URLs for external or third-party Internet websites referred to in this publication and does not guarantee that any content on such websites is, or will remain, accurate or appropriate.

Fordham University Press also publishes its books in a variety of electronic formats. Some content that appears in print may not be available in electronic books.

Library of Congress Cataloging-in-Publication Data

Lincoln and leadership : military, political, and religious decision making / edited by Randall M. Miller. — 1st ed.
    p. cm. — (The North's Civil War)
    Published in collaboration with the Abraham Lincoln Foundation of the Union League of Philadelphia.
    Includes bibliographical references and index.
    ISBN 978-0-8232-4344-0 (cloth : alk. paper) — ISBN 978-0-8232-4345-7 (pbk. : alk. paper)
    1. Lincoln, Abraham, 1809–1865. 2. Lincoln, Abraham, 1809–1865—Military leadership. 3. Lincoln, Abraham, 1809–1865—Ethics. 4. Political leadership—United States—History—19th century. 5. Presidents—United States—Decision making. 6. Leadership—United States—History—19th century. 7. United States—Politics and government—1861–1865—Decision making. 8. United States—Politics and government—1861–1865—Moral and ethical aspects. I. Miller, Randall M.
    E457.2.L817 2012
    973.7092—dc23

2011050441

Printed in the United States of America

14 13 12   5 4 3 2 1

First edition

Contents

Illustrations

Preface

This collection of essays derives from a conference on "Lincoln and Leadership," sponsored by the Abraham Lincoln Foundation of the Union League of Philadelphia and held on April 18, 2009, as part of the bicentennial of Lincoln's birth. The conference filled a large room to overflowing, as scholars, teachers, students, and the public crowded in for a day to hear presentations by prominent students of Lincoln on his role as commander in chief, as political helmsman, and as moral compass of the nation. The conference's three principal presentations have been revised and expanded, based on the many trenchant comments and questions of that April day and of subsequent readings by several scholars conversant with the issues. They are offered here as part of the ongoing, and still sometimes contentious, assessment of Lincoln's conduct, character, and consequence as president during the "ordeal by fire" that was the Civil War. And they are intended to invite new inquiry into considerations of Lincoln the public man and the meaning of his leadership.

The topic of Lincoln and leadership demanded attention in 2009 in light of the many different interests claiming him as the exemplar of managerial "best practices" and enlightened policy in fields as varied as politics, business, and social justice. And the Lincoln moment had come at what seemed to many a providential, or at least comparable, historical moment. The election of Barack Obama as president of the United States in 2008 recalled the rise of that other lanky lawyer from Illinois, who had also served only briefly in the U.S. Congress prior to his nomination and election to the presidency during a time of dire national crisis. Indeed, during the 2008 campaign Obama and his followers often invoked the memory of Lincoln—to inspire their following, and to suggest that experience in Washington was not a necessary prerequisite for success as head of state. During the period of transition as president-elect and at his inauguration, Obama quickened that theme. The likeness to Lincoln was worth cultivating as his administration faced its own crises. Calling up supposed Lincoln precedents and parallels continues in arguing for and against policy, both inside and outside the government. And both political parties claim his ideas and mythology for their own purposes.

At the same time, and indeed for some time, business consultants and college professors were using Lincoln as a case study in practical management. The popularity of Doris Kearns Goodwin's oft-cited book *Team of Rivals* (2005), which cast Lincoln as the adroit assembler of a cabinet of contenders whom he managed with skill to the nation's profit, added to the general idea that Lincoln knew his stuff. "Follow Lincoln's lead" has become the mantra for success in both the public and private sector.

Withal, Lincoln already was etched in the American mind as the "great man," even a god, who led the country through its own valley of the shadow of death. On his marbled throne in the Lincoln Memorial, he looked down on his people and gave them hope and courage to confront their worst crises. Father Abraham, after all, had saved the Union and promised the nation "a new birth of freedom." Lincoln the leader thus ensured that the great experiment in self-government would continue, in his words, as "the last best hope of earth." Countless Americans have made the pilgrimage to the Lincoln Memorial to be so inspired. That from the perspective of the Lincoln Memorial one might see across the Mall to the Capitol serves also to suggest that Lincoln keeps a watchful eye on the government for which he gave his "last full measure."

Within such a context, the conference on "Lincoln and Leadership" investigated three interlocking aspects of Lincoln's leadership by examining three critical decision-making problems that defined Lincoln's leadership. Its purpose was not to debunk or celebrate Lincoln's leadership but, rather, to understand its foundations and functioning. The chapters herein thus respectively consider Lincoln as the commander in chief developing as a military strategist and architect of a "hard war" policy; as the head of the Republican Party and the war president using patronage and psychology to get the nomination and win his reelection bid in 1864, in order to ensure a vigorous prosecution of the war and to secure emancipation; and as the nation's "theologian" and moral conscience struggling to make sense of God's will in letting the war continue, and in his Second Inaugural Address, making the case for humility in victory and Providence in history. Taken together, the chapters suggest the interplay of military, political, and religious factors informing Lincoln's thought and action, and guiding the dynamics and direction of his leadership.

The numerous images of Lincoln and the war reproduced herein also reinforce these themes. Lincoln was among the most photographed and drawn public figures of the century, and lithographs of battles, photographs of soldiers and after-battle scenes, political cartoons, and illustrated newspapers brought the war home to contemporaries with a potency and frequency no previous struggle approached. They also created an iconography of battles and leaders that informed thinking about Lincoln and others thereafter. The afterword to this book by Allen C. Guelzo reminds us of the qualities that made Lincoln the embodiment of the successful democratic leader, suggests ways to think about issues raised in the book, and points toward new lines of inquiry.

In sum, this book shows that even amid the cascade of Lincoln studies, there is something new to learn about him by looking closely at his decision making and by understanding that no single aspect of his leadership stood in isolation. Insomuch as this book encourages and informs further inquiry into the manner and matter of Lincoln and leadership, it also might suggest ways that the Lincoln of history remains vital to the issues of leadership today.

The book is yet another product of the scholarly and civic work of The Union League of Philadelphia. It represents as much a tribute to the Union League in its interests now as it also recalls the origins of the League in 1862 to promote Lincoln, liberty, and the Union. The conference and this book also fit the Union League's important new venture, The Heritage Center, which opened in June 2011. This institution brings together the Union League's own significant resources, as well as the library and archives of the former Civil War Library and Museum of Philadelphia and the Military Order of the Loyal Legion of the United States, for the study of the American Civil War, and provides space for exhibits and programs.

Even a book as short as this owes its success to many hands. First, the leadership of John Meko and Lucy Beard of the Abraham Lincoln Foundation of the Union League of Philadelphia demonstrated what intelligent design and delivery could do, in both conceiving a fine conference and supporting the publication of this book. Throughout the process, they raised financial, institutional, and general public support for this project.

At the Union League, James Mundy made further important contributions to the program in its conception and presentation. At the "Lincoln and Leadership" symposium, he gave an engaging and informative lunchtime talk, titled "Lincoln, the League, and Philadelphia." He also led tours of the Union League to show samples of its documentary and material culture collections. His help in framing Lincoln has been invaluable.

Also essential to the conception and direction of the symposium was the work of Barbara Mitnick. An accomplished scholar of American art, she introduced the session with an instructive presentation on the ways Lincoln was represented in art and images after his death. She pointed especially to the paintings at the Union League as emblematic of the deification of Lincoln in the public mind. She further informed the symposium and this book by taking notes from the question-and-answer period, which the authors of the chapters considered in revising their work. Her copious notes and her own comments sharpened the issues of Lincoln and leadership.

Various scholars have read all or parts of this book and offered useful suggestions as to revision, correction, and direction. Paul Cimbala supported the book from his first reading and invited it into his series at Fordham University Press on the North in the Civil War. David H. Burton, Robert F. Engs, Rayna Goldfarb, Stanley Harrold, Linda Patterson Miller, John M. Mulder, Katherine A. S. Sibley, and John David Smith read the introduction and made many useful suggestions, much to its profit. The late Phillip Shaw Paludan listened to my takes on our sixteenth president and suggested ways of thinking about Lincoln and leadership that informed my participation in planning the symposium and writing the introduction to this book. Almost a decade ago, the late Peter J. Parish responded to my readings of Lincoln and the war and suggested that a long look at Lincoln and leadership would repay the effort. It took some time to realize that promise. Robert Engs added to my knowledge of Lincoln and the war, through our collaboration on a book on the early Republican Party and our lunchtime discussions after that, talks that helped direct my own inquiries about Lincoln and leadership. James M. McPherson read and commented on the chapters with his usual insight and masterful knowledge of Lincoln. The Press's outside reviewers—Michael Birkner and Paul Escott—provided cogent and helpful reviews of the entire manuscript that did much to sharpen its focus and temper its arguments. Any errors that persist after such readings are our own.

The "Lincoln and Leadership" symposium was made possible by a grant from the National Endowment for the Humanities. At the NEH, Bruce Cole especially supported the award, believing that the symposium spoke to an important dimension of Lincoln's life and meaning during the bicentennial of his birth.

At Fordham University Press, Fredric Nachbaur has been consistently patient and encouraging as the book worked through the review process. His own leadership at the Press echoes the themes in this book. Also, Will Cerbone and Eric Newman guided the review and production process with skill and grace. All of them did much to make this book work.

To all, many thanks for making Lincoln come alive again.

Lincoln and Leadership

1   Lincoln and Leadership: An Introduction

Randall M. Miller

O ver a half-century ago, the eminent historian David Donald observed that Americans have been trying to "get right with Lincoln" since his death and predicted that trying to do so would continue thereafter.[1] He was right on both counts, as any sampling of the enormous and continuing cascade of literature on the man and his meaning will attest. Donald wrote and many others have agreed that Americans' preoccupation, or at least fascination, with getting to know Lincoln was in part due to the centrality of Lincoln and the events of his day in defining "freedom" and defending the integrity of the democratic experiment in self-government. Then, too, Lincoln's "martyrdom," as his assassination on Good Friday, April 14, 1865, came to be seen by countless Americans from his day to ours, seemed an affirmation of the American conceit about its supposed chosen place in God's grand design for human betterment. Through Lincoln might come America's "redemption," if the people would but understand him and follow his lead.

But which Lincoln should the people follow? In the public mind, Lincoln became over time the Great Emancipator, the Savior of the Union, the Man of the People, and more. The Lincoln Memorial—with Abraham the father seated on his throne and the holy scripture of his Gettysburg Address and Second Inaugural Address inscribed on the walls inside that great temple—put in marble the commanding presence of Lincoln, overseeing all. It was more than just convenience, a grand vista, and access to much open space on the Mall that has made the Lincoln Memorial a mecca for advocates and protesters of any number of causes. To stand before Lincoln, addressing an assembled people, was to claim for a cause the authority of God's own anointed son. Lincoln could, and did, become all things for many different people in the United States and abroad.[2]

But Lincoln the man was and has remained a puzzle. He was, for example, at once a man more committed to solving problems than espousing an ideology, a man with a clear purpose but no fixed policies to realize it. Lincoln's "continuing vogue," Donald rightly noted, was "his essential ambiguity."[3] It remains so today.

That essential ambiguity complicates any assessment of Lincoln's leadership. He was a man of enormous self-confidence, which, in time, led him to rely on his own judgment about military strategy, political management, and public speeches and letters, but he also was a man of remarkable humility, which led him to appreciate others' needs and sufferings and to keep his personal preferences secondary to public priorities. He was an enigma in a religious age, for he professed no particular religion even as he was steeped in biblical reading and wisdom and invoked Providence to explain his and America's place in history and the nation's possible redemption from its sins, especially slavery. He believed in people's capacity and inclination to see and do good, even as he explained that an American "house divided" over slavery in the 1850s was one heading toward ruin, because of a "slave power" conspiracy and proslavery Democrats corrupting the political process by numbing people's moral sensibilities. And he was someone who believed fundamentally that a nation must be grounded in moral principles that demanded respect for law and humanity, but he worried over the prospects of either in an intemperate age. Lincoln's ready, and sometimes ribald, humor provided relief for himself and often good relations with colleagues in government and visitors begging favors, but it also disguised what Lincoln's law partner termed his "melancholy" and his exhaustion and anguish over the relentless demands of war.[4]

For all that, Lincoln was unambiguous where it counted. Perhaps his greatest genius was his uncommon ability never to lose sight of or confuse priorities. No priority stood higher than saving the Union, as Lincoln repeatedly reminded people in speeches, writings, and personal conversations. He seized any opportunity to make that case. Thus, for example, in late August 1862, when the war was going badly, Lincoln wrote a public letter to make clear his and the nation's purpose—to save the Union. He was responding to the criticisms of Horace Greeley, editor of the influential *New York Tribune*, who claimed that Union victory demanded that Lincoln step up enforcement of congressional acts against slavery and make the war one to end slavery. In his August 22, 1862, reply, Lincoln wrote that he would leave no one in doubt as to his policy to save the Union in "the shortest way under the Constitution." He stated the priority clearly: "My paramount object in this struggle *is* to save the Union, and is *not* either to save or destroy slavery." He would do so by freeing the slaves, keeping slavery intact, or freeing some slaves and letting others remain in bondage, according to any power that he had to do anything and depending on which policy promised to deliver the Union. He closed his letter by noting that his "*official* duty" did not

"Abraham Lincoln," photograph by Mathew Brady, 1860. After achieving national attention because of his debates with Stephen A. Douglas in the 1858 senatorial campaign in Illinois, Lincoln moved onto a larger stage among Republicans. Lincoln was very conscious in developing his image, which especially included carefully crafting his speeches and his presentation in photographs. He appreciated the power of the photograph and posed as a statesman, family man, or commander in chief, as necessary. As part of "presenting" himself to eastern Republicans in 1860 at the Cooper Union in New York City, he had this photograph taken. The image and his speech gained widespread currency, the former through engravings and lithographs and the latter through printings. (Library of Congress)

modify his "oft-expressed *personal* wish that all men every where could be free."[5] But leadership demanded that he understand, and make understood, and then act on and for the nation's best interest, not his own.

Implicit in this was Lincoln's recognition that by keeping the objective of saving the Union first, he was assured of more general support from the public than by pressing for emancipation as the principal war aim. As he observed in September 1861, it was necessary to move cautiously on the slavery question because of the need to hold the loyalty of the border states, where slavery was legal and loyalty to the Union conditional. He therefore revoked an emancipation order issued by General John C. Fremont in his military district because Fremont's action, though popular with Radical Republicans, endangered the larger war effort. To lose Kentucky, he wrote, "is nearly the same as to lose the whole game. Kentucky gone, we can not hold Missouri, nor, as I think, Maryland. These all against us, and the job on our hands is too large for us. We would as well consent to separation at once, including the surrender of this capitol."[6] For Lincoln, political realities mattered much in shaping policy and strategy. Any premature effort to make emancipation a war aim would lose the war. And if the Union failed, there surely would be no emancipation.

The prospect for emancipation hinged on Union victory. In fact, when Lincoln wrote his letter to Greeley, he already had committed to issuing the preliminary emancipation proclamation as a war measure, which he did in September 1862. But leadership demanded preparing the public mind for such a radical policy and making clear the necessity of it, always within the context of serving and saving the Union.

Lincoln understood that the power and appeal of the concept of "Union" was no abstraction. Although the Federal government hardly touched people's lives before the Civil War, the Union was palpable to Americans as the embodiment of a collective thrust toward freedom to make one's own way, acquire property, and enjoy the fruits of honest labor—whether working a farm, making a cabinet, carrying produce to market, or any other productive activity. The United States was the nation that promised human betterment. It was, as Lincoln stated, following Thomas Jefferson's phrasing, "the last best hope of earth."

The term "Union," as the historian Elizabeth Varon recently observed, in Lincoln's day had "a transcendent, mystical quality as the object" of people's "patriotic devotion and civic religion." It "called to mind the geographic, linguistic, cultural, and historical bonds that held America's citizenry together." The Union was the land of opportunity, the proof that government based on the authority

"Inauguration Day, March 4, 1861," photograph by Alexander Gardner. A mass of people, reported to be the largest crowd to witness an inauguration, gathered at the steps of the unfinished U.S. Capitol building to see Lincoln's swearing in. Although few people could hear his Inaugural Address, they read it soon enough in the papers and argued over its meaning as to where Lincoln stood on using any means necessary to end the crisis. (Library of Congress)

of ballots, not bullets or bayonets, could succeed, and the counterpoint to all the autocracy, corruption, and misery of the Old World. Thus any effort to destroy it—"disunion"—must be resisted, lest all hope for a democratic republic be lost.[7] Lincoln drew from that deep well of love for Union and fear for its failure to explain why the Union must be saved at all costs. No theme echoed more in his writings and speeches than that divine calling of saving the Union.

Lincoln's constant calls to defend the Union emphasized the vital connection between Union and freedom. He especially pointed to the obligation to honor and fulfill the promise of the American Revolution, and in doing so gave the cause for Union renewed energy and purpose. In his First Inaugural Address, on March 4, 1861, for example, Lincoln reminded Americans that the Union—the nation—was born in the American Revolution and was older than the Constitution, and that it was inextricably bound together by law, history, common sense, and destiny. He also warned that the world was watching the United States and its experiment in self-government, so that any failure of its "union" bode ill for liberty everywhere. He closed that speech with a call to reclaim and regain that common heritage binding all Americans. Thus came his famous peroration: "The mystic chords of memory, stretching from every battle-field, and patriot grave, to every living heart and hearthstone, all over this broad land, will yet swell the chorus of the Union, when again touched, as surely they will be, by the better of angels of our nature." Again, as he stated in his December 3, 1861, message to Congress, "the insurrection is largely, if not exclusively, a war upon the first principle of popular government—the rights of the people." The "great task" facing the United States was clear: "The struggle of today, is not altogether for today—it is for a vast future also."[8]

When the interests of winning the war against the disunionists dictated the death of slavery, Lincoln in his annual message of December 1, 1862, explained to Congress why it had become necessary to move against the "peculiar institution." He averred that "without slavery the rebellion could never have existed; without slavery it could not continue." And he declared that the way to victory was clear: "We *say* we are for the Union. . . . We know how to save the Union. The world knows we do know how to save it. We—even *we here*—hold the power, and bear the responsibility. In *giving* freedom to the *slave*, we *assure* freedom to the *free*—honorable alike in what we give, and what we preserve." He concluded that if the Union honored its commitment to freedom and self-preservation, which now demanded emancipation, "the world will forever applaud, and God must forever bless" the United States. Most famously, in his Gettysburg Address Lincoln fused the Revolutionary lineage of the promise of freedom with "a new birth of freedom" and the divine duty to complete "the unfinished work" of winning the war, so that democratic government would survive.[9]

The Union and all its promise were unconditional and would never be surrendered. The obligations it entailed were both immediate and perpetual. It required will, resolve, and sacrifice. It required flexibility as to means without any concession as to ends. Lincoln would negotiate with the Confederacy on prisoner exchanges and like matters and even entertain proposals for ending the fighting, but he was adamant that such discussions were always premised on the convic-

A Council of War in '61 (New York, 1866), engraving by H. B. Hall and G. E. Perine. After the war Lincoln's status as commander in chief was burnished by many images of him as a strong leader, often standing alone. This engraving shows Lincoln in a more receptive mode, listening to the advice of General Winfield Scott and others in planning strategy. It fairly captures Lincoln's willingness early in the war to consider the advice of military men. (Library of Congress)

tion that the Union was indivisible and, after emancipation became policy, that freedom was irrevocable.

It was in that context of unwavering commitment to saving the Union that Lincoln finally moved against slavery. In his method, he showed his ability as a leader to adjust to new circumstances, even to create them, without sacrificing basic principles. To be sure, Lincoln did not act alone or control events. Pressure from Republicans in Congress enacting laws to weaken slavery when and where it directly aided the rebellion, to keep it out of U.S. territories, and to end it outright in the District of Columbia—all pushed Lincoln toward accepting emancipation as a war aim. So, too, calls from northern Protestant ministers and congregations and others to free the slaves in order to win God's favor could not be dismissed altogether, though Lincoln never supposed that any clergyman or president knew the will of God so completely as the ministers petitioning him to declare for abolition assumed. And the slaves themselves made the case for emancipation by fleeing bondage at every opportunity as the Union armies advanced, as planters left their holdings to fight, and as authority broke down across the South. Blacks, enslaved and free, offered their services to the Union cause, and although rebuffed early in the war, such acts of patriotism could not be ignored. In time, manpower needs dictated enlisting blacks in the army. All this, and more, changed the context in which thinking about slavery and its relationship to winning the war developed.[10]

As the necessity of ending slavery—the cause of the war and a strength of the rebellion—became ever more evident, Lincoln sought to settle the possibility in the public mind before acting on it. In September 1861 and again in May 1862, Lincoln reversed the orders of two of his commanders—the antislavery generals John C. Fremont and David Hunter, respectively—to end slavery within their military districts. He did so insisting that any such order was the prerogative of the president alone as a war measure or of Congress as a legislative one. In these cases, Lincoln reminded his critics that military men were not to make public policy. But he also noted that such pressures against slavery from soldiers in the field pointed to the way war was changing supposedly protected institutions.

Lincoln was sometimes vague in public as to the direction of his thinking regarding emancipation, or he avoided the question rather than commit to a specific plan or timetable. He seemed to concede the initiative to others or to events, even to fate. Consequently, some people viewed him as unprincipled or weak. In 1861 into 1862, he sent a mixed message on where he stood regarding Congress's antislavery actions. He did so most notably in 1862 when he signed the Second Confiscation Act, which freed any Rebel-owned slaves who came within Union lines, but he sent a draft veto message to Congress explaining his misgivings about the law's constitutionality regarding the confiscation of property. Lincoln's message served more to irritate Republicans than inform the public.

Overall, however, Lincoln anticipated that slavery's end was coming, and he promised no special obligation or effort to save the South's "peculiar institution," unless doing so served the interests of the Union. No doubt in part to win over southern unionists as well as to acknowledge the direction the war likely would go, Lincoln in his December 3, 1861, message to Congress warned, "In considering the policy to be adopted for suppressing the insurrection, I have been anxious and careful that the inevitable conflict for this purpose shall not degenerate into a violent and remorseless revolutionary struggle." He sought to keep the integrity of the Union "the primary object of the contest," but he could not control events.[11]

As the forces for ending slavery swelled, Lincoln noted the inexorable march toward emancipation by offering alternative ways to address the problem of slavery. He proposed a plan for compensated emancipation to induce border state and "loyal" slaveholders to give up slavery voluntarily, as a prelude to a larger policy that would respect "property rights" while removing the moral and economic drag of human bondage. Lincoln supported colonization schemes to settle blacks in Haiti or Africa, because he believed most whites would never tolerate the emancipation of slaves if it meant having to accept the mass of un-propertied "black" people into the republic to compete for work and place. The failures of such schemes worked in part to make clear that emancipation, if it came, would have to accommodate ex-slaves in some way within the country. Whether Lincoln was responding to perceived public opinion, and his own views on race, in persisting with colonization schemes, even after 1863, or carefully conditioning the public mind to the impossibility of such a policy is a question that nagged his contemporaries and the historians after them. If the motive is unclear, the effect was not: emancipation would proceed without any forced colonization. And events were pushing toward emancipation.[12]

All this showed Lincoln as cautious and careful regarding emancipation. Any such move, he believed, must help win the war. Still, in considering Lincoln's thinking on the subject, it is significant that he signed the laws that ended slavery in the territories and in the District of Columbia. He also made a strong symbolic statement about the wrong of slavery in 1862 when he refused the petitions of several prominent individuals to stay the execution of Nathaniel Gordon, an American convicted of international slave trading; Gordon was the only individual to suffer the full consequence of an American law forbidding such trade on American ships. In sum, from 1861 to the preliminary emancipation proclamation in 1862, Lincoln had kept alive the possibility that slavery would be a necessary casualty of the war. And in 1862, when he issued the preliminary emancipation proclamation following the Union victory at Antietam, Lincoln warned that abolition would come to those slaveholders who persisted in supporting disunion.

The Emancipation Proclamation that Lincoln issued on New Year's Day 1863 "freed" all slaves still in areas of rebellion on and after that day. In issuing and

President Lincoln, Writing the Proclamation of Freedom, January 1, 1863 (Cincinnati,
1863), colored lithograph by Ehrgott, Forbriger and Co., after a painting by David
Gilmour Blythe. A common motif in rendering Lincoln drafting the Emancipation
Proclamation was that he was divinely inspired in the task. The extent to which
appeals from antislavery clergy and laity affected Lincoln's decision for emancipation is not known, and the proclamation read as a legal document rather than a
prophecy or sermon; but the image of a pensive Lincoln with a Bible and a Constitution in his lap, as rendered in this popular lithograph, gained popular currency,
especially after Lincoln's "martyr" death in 1865. (Library of Congress)

later defending the Emancipation Proclamation, Lincoln justified his extraordinary act of executive assertion "as a fit and necessary war measure for suppressing said rebellion," and "an act of justice, warranted by the Constitution, upon
military necessity." Although presented as a war measure, the proclamation was
revolutionary in its intent and prospect. Its dry legal language belied its pur-

pose, for it was an unequivocal national commitment to abolition. Contemporaries understood that in 1863. In practical terms, the proclamation meant that every advance of Union armies was an advance for freedom. Slavery's future was doomed insomuch as the Union's future was saved. As noted in Lincoln's day, the success of the proclamation would effectively end slavery in the United States, for if slavery died in the Lower South, it could not survive in the border slave states.

In reacting to the new policy, Democrats beat up on Lincoln and the Republicans as radicals bent on destroying property rights, encouraging all manner of outrages by "emancipated" blacks, and threatening any prospect of reunion. Meanwhile, Republicans, abolitionists, and blacks hailed the proclamation as ensuring God's favor and Union victory, and freeing the nation to grow and stand as liberty's champion in the world. Lincoln accepted the "costs" because he appreciated the reward emancipation promised in saving the Union. He summed up the reason for the new policy neatly in 1864 when, in defending the Emancipation Proclamation, he stated that "the moment came when . . . slavery must die that the nation might live."[13]

Once Lincoln committed to emancipation as policy, whether out of military, diplomatic, moral, or other necessity, or combinations thereof, he never retreated from it. It had become a priority. As such, it was nonnegotiable, and it became a condition for any peace with those rebelling against the Union—however much they were newly galvanized against the Union because of that policy. The nation was ready for emancipation and needed it. But Lincoln feared that the end of the war might remove the constitutional cover for emancipation, so he pressed for an amendment to secure the policy. Ever the lawyer and realist, Lincoln wanted the fact of freedom clearly stated and protected under the Constitution. To drive home his own commitment to emancipation, Lincoln took the unusual step of signing the proposed Thirteenth Amendment when it came to his desk. The amendment was, he said, "a King's cure for all the evils." The Union would have that "new birth of freedom" heralded in the Gettysburg Address by inscribing it in the sacred document as a national responsibility.[14]

Emancipation as policy and national obligation reflected Lincoln's and the Republicans' acceptance of a concept that political scientists later termed "positive liberty." It was an idea that some abolitionists, and others, held that regarded the nation-state as an instrument to expand liberty, rather than government being a threat to freedom (as was the common view among Americans since the Revolution).[15] Lincoln never articulated a fully developed argument for the nation-state as the "custodian of freedom" or the "guardian of liberty," as did some

Writing the Emancipation Proclamation (Baltimore, ca. 1864), etching by Adalbert Johann Volck. Southerners and northern Copperheads saw Lincoln as a satanic madman trampling the Constitution and inciting racial chaos, as in this widely reprinted etching of Lincoln dipping in the Devil's inkstand to pen what his critics regarded as heresy. (Library of Congress)

Radical Republicans who wanted to assert Federal power to secure and protect basic civil rights for newly freed slaves. But he was moving in that direction in his own thinking. Lincoln stated the case explicitly in 1864 when responding to criticism about emancipation and an increased Federal power. He wrote that the "world has never had a good definition of liberty, and the American people are just now in want of one." But, as Lincoln continued, likening the nation-state to a shepherd, the "shepherd drives the wolf from the sheep's throat, for which the sheep thanks the shepherd as a *liberator*, while the wolf denounces him for the same act as the destroyer of liberty, especially as the sheep is a black one. Plainly the sheep and the wolf are not agreed on a definition of the word liberty; and precisely the same difference prevails to-day among us human creatures, even in the North, and all professing to love liberty."[16] With the Thirteenth Amendment, Republicans and Lincoln committed the nation to positive liberty by ending slavery and, in the second clause of the amendment, expressly empowering the Congress "to enforce this article [prohibiting slavery] with appropriate legislation." This was the first time such enabling power had been included in a constitutional amendment, and its implication and obligation were to use the power of the nation-state to define, defend, and even direct that freedom.[17]

First Reading of the Emancipation Proclamation of President Lincoln (np, [1864]), print based on a painting by Francis Bicknell Carpenter. This popular print was based on a large painting by Carpenter, who had stayed in the White House for six months working on projects and gained Lincoln's confidence. It places Lincoln and his proclamation at the center of vision and implies a unity and serenity among cabinet members that belied the real tensions among them, though the rendering portends the rivalry with Salmon P. Chase by having him standing, arms folded, ominously behind Lincoln. (Library of Congress)

Emancipation as policy and promise also led to the recruitment of blacks as soldiers in what became an army of freedom. Lincoln accepted Congress's call for such troops, understanding that enlisting black men for military service would not only meet pressing manpower needs in a war of staggering casualty rates but also give blacks a rightful claim to the liberty their service would secure. The rallying of blacks to the flag, the successful recruitment of slaves, and the heroic service of the "colored troops" removed any doubts Lincoln might have had about the wisdom of bringing blacks into the army, an act even more revolutionary and repulsive in white southerners' eyes than the Emancipation Proclamation itself. As president, Lincoln stood firm that black soldiers were to be regarded as U.S. soldiers, and declared that any Confederate refusal to treat them as such if they were captured would bring retaliation. He regarded black soldiers as men. As he stated firmly in April 1864, following accounts of the Fort Pillow Massacre of black soldiers, "Having determined to use the negro as a soldier, there is no way but to give him all the protection given to any other soldier."[18]

When Democrats and others persisted in complaining that arming blacks was tantamount to inviting a race war—or at least giving blacks an unwarranted sense of being "equal" to whites—Lincoln spoke out in defense of blacks' service. He did so most famously and forcefully in a public letter that was read first at a Union rally in Springfield, Illinois, in August 1863, again at a mass meeting in New York City one month after the antiblack riots there, and then published in the *New York Times*, where it gained national attention. Lincoln began by acknowledging fundamental differences between himself and the critics of the new emancipation and enlistment policies, noting, "I certainly wish that all men could be free, while I suppose you do not," and continued by defending his constitutional authority in issuing the Proclamation and the necessity and utility of enlisting blacks in the army. He went to the heart of matter when he stated, "You say you will not fight to free negroes. Some of them seem willing to fight for you; but, no matter. Fight you, then, exclusively to save the Union. I issued the proclamation on purpose to aid you in saving the Union. Whenever you shall have conquered all resistance to the Union, if I shall urge you to continue fighting, it will be an apt time, then, for you to declare you will not fight to free negroes." Almost mocking the critics who opposed emancipation and black enlistments, he concluded, "I thought that whatever negroes can be got to do as soldiers, leaves just so much less for white soldiers to do, in saving the Union. Does it appear otherwise to you? But negroes, like other people, act upon motives. Why should they do any thing for us, if we will do nothing for them? If they stake their lives for us, they must be prompted by the strongest motive—even the promise of freedom. And the promise being made, must be kept." In this argument, Lincoln appealed to self-interest, which he always believed animated men to act, and to right, which he always believed defined men as moral beings. He also framed the issue, again, in terms of putting the Union first as the bonding agent that would secure freedom for all.[19]

Because Lincoln viewed preserving the Union as his principal sworn responsibility as president, he put aside almost all other executive functions in order to focus on winning the war. He spent his days as commander in chief reading military reports and telegraph messages, looking over maps, and corresponding with generals regarding strategy and even tactics. He seemed hardly to worry about other domestic issues, except for political management, and he left domestic policy almost wholly to his cabinet members and to Congress to manage. This was easy to do because Lincoln and the Republicans were of one mind on domestic policy. They shared in the Republican belief in "free soil, free labor, and free men" that had become the party mantra and that embodied Lincoln's own life story. As a westerner, he understood the importance of government aid to improve transportation on land and on water—what was then called "internal improvements"—and as a Whig legislator in Illinois and a lawyer for railroads, he had argued for the necessity of support to promote the social and economic health and wealth of the nation. Lincoln even had developed and patented a device to lift river craft over shoals by means of "adjustable buoyant air chambers." "Improvement" was a word Lincoln repeated throughout his life, for it bespoke his fundamental belief about the possibility of human progress by means of discovery and invention. In his annual messages to Congress, he encouraged legislation on internal improvements, building a transcontinental railroad, a generous immigration policy, a homestead bill, the creation of a Department of Agriculture, support for science and technology, land-grant colleges, and other measures that advanced the Republican Party's interest in opening the West to settlement and development. That meant using government to make it possible for honest men to get ahead by having better and more reliable information, access to useful education, and the means to engage in the market economy. In sum, such governmental action promised to help the thrifty, honest, and industrious people to improve their lot in life. In all this, Lincoln was endorsing Republican policies that promised that the future would be better than the past. This was itself a war measure, for it meant that winning the war and saving the Union would repay the sacrifice in blood and treasure Americans were making.[20]

As a war president, however, he begrudged the Congress little role in shaping military policy, which led to unnecessary distrust and misunderstandings between Congress and president and likely stirred Republican leaders in the Congress to more vigilance than they otherwise might have practiced. Lincoln acted unilaterally to meet crises and left it to Congress to sustain his actions. Most dramatically in defining his relationship with Congress from the outset of his presidency, he did not call the Congress into special session after the firing on Fort Sumter in April 1861; rather, on his own authority he called for seventy-five thousand militia to put down the rebellion. Likewise, he suspended habeas corpus on his own authority. When the new, Republican-controlled Congress convened in July 1861, it "ratified" Lincoln's actions. And the die was cast.[21]

But as the war progressed, some Republicans and virtually all Democrats thought such unilateral executive acts went beyond Lincoln's constitutional power. The Republican-controlled Congress invariably endorsed Lincoln's actions, but he and his party paid a political price after Democrats charged Lincoln and the Republicans with usurpation of power and the destruction of civil liberties. Lincoln as tyrant became a common political motif in image and invective, and Lincoln never wholly shook off the charge during the war or even in history. Nor did he seem to care, for he persisted in acting on his own authority when he believed necessity demanded it. As he explained in a June 1863 letter regarding his decision to suspend the writ of habeas corpus in response to antiwar activity, such action was "indispensable to the public safety" and necessary to prevent interference with the nation's defense during "a clear, flagrant, and gigantic case of Rebellion." The suspension was temporary and conditional, in response to extraordinary circumstances, but nonetheless troubling to defenders of civil liberties then and thereafter.[22]

Lincoln chafed at congressional efforts to direct military policy and practice. This was especially the case after Republicans created a Joint Committee on the Conduct of the War to review the conduct and character of generals and other military matters. Congressional Republicans also criticized the executive management of the war, especially the corrupt and inefficient purchasing practices of Secretary of War Simon Cameron, a Pennsylvanian supposedly forced on Lincoln as a condition of his getting the presidential nomination, and someone whose political machinations got Cameron as many enemies as "friends." Such criticism, and the "shoddy" uniforms and other supplies for which Cameron's office had let out contracts, led Lincoln to replace Cameron with the more managerially

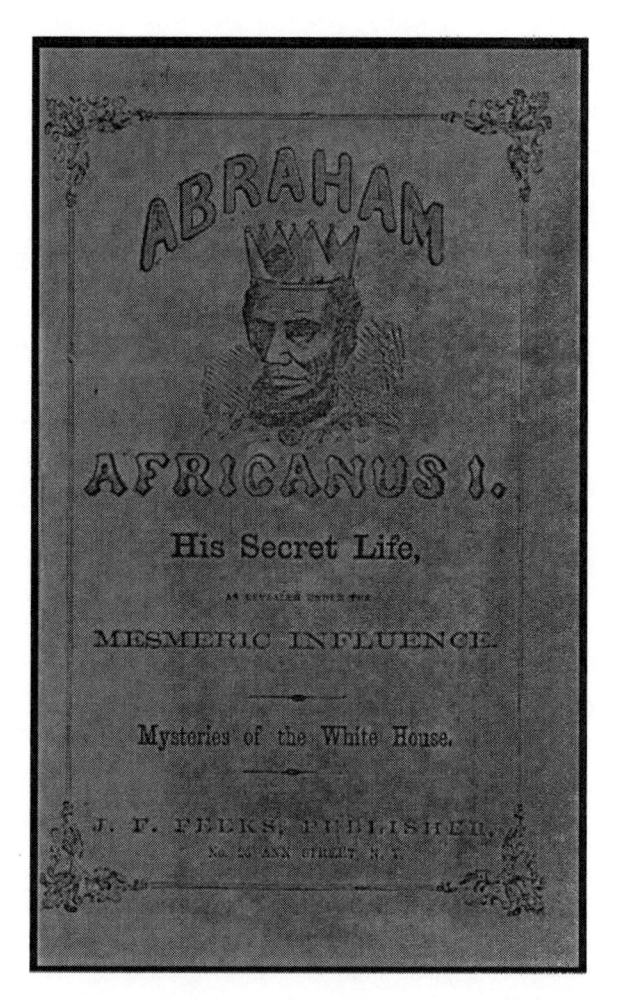

Abraham Africanus I, cover page of pamphlet (New York, 1864). Lincoln's emancipation policy, his suspension of habeas corpus in trying to suppress Copperheads and disruptions of recruitment, and his support of the Conscription Act all riled up opposition and, to Democrats anyway, made Lincoln a tyrant. Democrats used such fear to good effect politically, and charges that Lincoln abused his powers by such acts have continued among biographers, historians, and people using Lincoln as an example of presidential power even today. (Library of the University of Illinois at Urbana-Champaign)

rigorous and more radically Republican Edwin Stanton, an appointment that pleased Republicans in Congress.[23]

Also, regarding Reconstruction, Lincoln and congressional Republicans did not always agree on policy or responsibility. Lincoln considered the question of reforming and readmitting the seceded states his primary responsibility as an instrument of war policy. He also wanted flexibility in designing policies, which he called "experiments." He explained his thinking to Congress in 1863, in laying out his initial proposals regarding pardons and forming governments: "The objections to a premature presentation of a plan by the national Executive consists in the danger of committals on points which could be more safely left to further developments"; but, he continued, "saying that reconstruction will be accepted if presented in a specified way, it is not said that it will never be accepted in any other way." Congressional Republicans gave Lincoln leeway during the war but signaled their intention to assume a principal role in Reconstruction as the war wound down. They wanted sterner measures of loyalty from white southerners than Lincoln had proposed, and wanted to insure that only those unionist southerners who had demonstrated loyalism, and even suffered for it, had the upper hand in remaking a defeated South.[24]

The strains were most evident when Lincoln pocket-vetoed the Wade-Davis bill in 1864, which had provided for a strict test in recognizing "loyal" subjects in the seceded states who might participate in reestablishing and reforming the governments to be readmitted to the Union. Lincoln stated that he did so because he did not want to be bound by a single policy. Rather, as he explained, he preferred instead to conduct experiments in reconstruction, such as his earlier plan that would allow a seceded state seeking readmission to begin the process whenever a number of citizens equal to 10 percent of the number of people who voted in that state in the 1860 presidential election took a loyalty oath. Lincoln's plan was intended to encourage unionist sentiment in the South in order to undermine the Confederacy—a prospect that Lincoln always overestimated—but it gained almost no support in Congress. Lincoln acted unilaterally in that matter because he considered proposals for reconstruction as war measures as long as the war continued. Thus he tried to keep the prerogatives and initiative in his hands rather than yield to Congress, even one controlled by his own party.

With Union victory imminent in 1865, Lincoln seemed to turn more toward congressional Republicans' definitions of "loyalty" as the test for building new governments in seceded states. He also accepted congressional policy regarding the freed slaves, as in its creation of a Federal Freedmen's Bureau to take up matters of abandoned lands, aid for refugees, and getting the "freedmen" to work and protecting their right to make contracts on their own behalf. Lincoln also was moving toward the congressional Republicans' insistence that any "reconstructed" southern state must include a political place for black men, especially those who had served in the U.S. Army or had demonstrated their intelligence and learning. Indeed, in his last public address, two days after Robert E. Lee surrendered his army at Appomattox, Lincoln stated that he "would prefer that [the elective franchise] were now conferred" on just such men.[25] But Lincoln's thinking on Reconstruction and any new relationship with a postwar Congress was cut short by his assassination in April 1865, leaving it to Andrew Johnson (a lifelong Democrat), the Republican-controlled Congress, and the people in the former Confederacy to work out Reconstruction, all claiming, when convenient, that their actions accorded with the wishes and will of the now dead "Savior of the Union" and "Great Emancipator." During the time of his presidency, however, Lincoln jealously guarded his war powers from congressional intrusion, and a clear and effective postwar Reconstruction policy suffered for want of better presidential and congressional collaboration.

Lincoln's failure to lay out a clear path for Reconstruction reflected both his preoccupation with winning the war and his management style. On the latter count, Lincoln was haphazard and even undisciplined, a carryover from his days as a lawyer, when he was at best inattentive or indifferent to all the details of office management. In forming his cabinet, Lincoln selected various and competing political chieftains, both to satisfy the different factions within the Republican Party just then coming to office for the first time, and to bring talent into the government. Answering the question as to why he appointed ostensible political rivals, Lincoln observed that the nation "needed the strongest men of the party in the Cabinet," and that he "had no right to deprive the country of their services."[26] This statement reflected Lincoln's political astuteness, but his practice also invited "turf wars" within the cabinet. He got along well enough with most of the cabinet officers—largely by dealing with them individually rather than gathering them as a body, where competing interests and personalities clashed; and by giving department heads considerable freedom over the implementation and management of policies in their respective departments. Scholars disagree on the extent to which the appointments and arrangement succeeded, but there is no disputing that the method fit the man.[27]

When someone proved unsatisfactory, such as Simon Cameron, Lincoln eased him out of office; when someone proved overly ambitious and potentially disruptive of Lincoln's larger agenda, such as Salmon P. Chase in angling for the presidential nomination in 1864, Lincoln let him go. In both cases, Lincoln deftly handled the problems by finding new places for the men that kept them from losing face, removed them from the political process (Cameron to Russia as ambassador and Chase to the Supreme Court as Chief Justice), and also retained their service for the country in areas where they might do good. Appointing Chase as Chief Justice of the Supreme Court in December 1864, after the death of Lincoln's bête noire Roger B. Taney, was a brilliant move. Despite Lincoln's worries that Chase's "unbounded ambition" to become president might cause him to use the position to "intrigue to make himself President," the appointment both assuaged those Radical Republicans who had supported Chase's ill-fated effort to replace Lincoln, and assured that Republican wartime and Reconstruction policies would get a fair hearing if challenged in the courts.[28]

From the beginning of his presidency, Lincoln made clear that he was in control. Doing so tamped down rivalries, and also won him respect among initial doubters such as William Henry Seward that a backwoods lawyer could run the government. Lincoln consulted the cabinet early in his administration, when he was feeling his way as president, taking the measure of the men he had appointed, and also confronted with the explosive situation at Fort Sumter, where any precipitate action might start a war. Once the war came, Lincoln looked less to the cabinet collectively for advice. He involved himself where he thought his principal responsibility required his full attention, and he intervened little in departmental matters when he had confidence in the men he appointed. Some cabinet members and congressional Republicans complained about the lack of general meetings, but such practice suited Lincoln's personality and priorities. It also contributed to some disorder in management and confusion about policy, such as Reconstruction. Who spoke for the administration on that matter was not always clear. For example, the War and Treasury Departments set up different labor policies on the abandoned or confiscated lands of Rebels—practices that seemed to promise a Federal commitment to protection for the freedmen in working under contracts but lacking any explicit presidential endorsement.[29]

Lincoln also operated with only a small circle of advisers or sometimes no advisers at all. His friendship with Seward, which grew quickly after Lincoln demonstrated that he, Lincoln, and not Seward would run the government, was a special case. Lincoln conferred with friends in Congress, and he kept up correspondence with Republican governors, who informed him of recruitment needs, resistance to the draft, political leanings, and more. Early in the war, he sought counsel from military men, with very mixed and too often disappointing results, which led him to rely increasingly on his own readings of reports, study of military manuals and maps (Lincoln was a great map reader), and instincts in managing military affairs. Not until he found generals such as Ulysses S. Grant who shared his strategic vision, and who were not afraid to act on it, did Lincoln "trust" military men enough to let them have their way. He never developed a close friendship with any general. For all his many "friends" and correspondents, he was in modern parlance a "loner."[30]

The constant demands on Lincoln's time, and the poor management of that time, added to the problems. Lincoln received a constant stream of visitors, petitioners, and others begging for patronage positions, the appointment of a relative or friend to a military command or office, relief of some sort, the staying of an execution of a soldier who had run off or had committed some capital offense, and a host of other favors. Lincoln's secretaries sought to limit access, with some success by war's end, but Lincoln never cut himself off from such direct and frequent contact with "the public." Whether by design or default, it was for Lincoln a good way to stay informed about public concerns beyond reading the highly political press, and it made the president and what he represented knowable to the people. Such practice reflected Lincoln's lifelong habit of preferring to meet with people directly to get unfiltered information and to make his own case. Doing so earned people's trust because Lincoln listened to and considered their requests and explained his own position. It was, however, also inefficient and exhausting. The steady march of people took its toll. Lincoln was a tired president. Only his retreat to the Soldiers' Home—the cottage and grounds several miles from the White House—provided relief and uninterrupted time for Lincoln to think and write. Significantly, as the historian Matthew Pinsker has shown, much of Lincoln's best work was composed there, away from the crush of the government offices.[31]

Whatever his failings as an administrator, Lincoln succeeded as a party leader. From his first run for office at age twenty-three to his death, Lincoln was consumed by politics, the "engine" of his ambition. He believed that political participation was the lifeblood of a free, democratic society, and he participated vigorously in political matters as a candidate, as a campaigner for others, and as a political manager (even a "party boss" in Illinois Whig circles). Throughout his life he believed that democratic politics worked best within a party system. Political parties provided an effective means to identify and gather common interests and present them to the public forcefully, and they caused men to think in terms of cooperation, not just competition. Loyalty to a party was akin to loyalty to a church, for it showed where a man stood in any community. On all that, Lincoln was adamant. In his eulogy for Henry Clay in July 1852, Lincoln stated his fundamental principle that "a free people, in times of peace and quiet—when pressed by no common danger—naturally divide into parties. At such times, the man who is of neither party is not—cannot be, of any consequence."[32] He never retreated from that belief. One reason that Lincoln worried about the destructive tendencies of the "slave power" in the 1850s was that it had broken apart the Whig Party and threatened orderly political life altogether by undermining the party system. Party politics, conducted openly and honestly, strengthened the nation. Their absence invited chaos and tyranny.[33]

Lincoln worked hard to insure the health of the Republican Party so that it might represent the interests of its supporters fairly in elections and in office. For that reason, he spent much time as president-elect and early in his presidency doling out political patronage. He did so thinking that it was especially important to appoint the right men to offices from cabinet posts down to postmasterships as a reward for services rendered or needed, and to insure that the party the people had elected would be able to honor its pledges by making and implementing policy. Lincoln kept a close watch on party doings and corresponded regularly with Republicans regarding patronage, candidates, and party platforms. He understood that effective party management and success in elections were essential to winning the war.

Lincoln as political leader also knew he needed to go beyond partisanship to maintain support for the war. He especially did not want people to identify the war solely as a Republican obligation. Thus, for example, he found places for Democratic and ethnic-group chieftains in the army so that their followers would support the war effort. Doing so angered and frustrated some Republicans and several generals. The former worried about creating Democratic war heroes who might challenge Republicans at the polls, and the latter worried about creating command problems by being saddled with ambitious politicians eager to win glory but knowing little about military affairs. The blunders of several of Lincoln's appointees in the field cost him politically in particular cases, but the overall practice did expand political support for the war effort.

Also, in trying to build a Union coalition that would have wide appeal, even in the postwar South, Lincoln thought in terms of bringing in erstwhile Democrats to improve the Republicans' chances. He did so most notably in the 1864 election with the addition of Andrew Johnson, a lifelong Democrat and unionist from Tennessee, to the presidential ticket and the rebranding of the Republicans as the

Union Party. In doing so, however, Lincoln did not abandon his commitment to party politics. Rather, he was recasting the party to meet new demands and to insure its success with voters.

The critical moment for Lincoln's political leadership came in 1864. Casualty rates had reached staggering levels with the practice of "hard war" and General Ulysses S. Grant's dogged, and ultimately successful, practice of making the campaign a continuous battle to wear down and finally destroy Lee's army. Lincoln supported the strategy but worried about the political price. Democrats had made significant inroads during the war by playing on people's frustrations with a seeming military stalemate. In state elections in 1862 and 1863 they also had gained at the polls by raising fears that Lincoln's emancipation policy would excite racial unrest and even miscegenation—a word invented in 1863 to trade on concerns that "free" blacks would ravish white women and, as Democrats claimed, that Republicans would encourage interracial unions. Democrats had fared well, too, by casting Lincoln as a tyrant because of the suspension of habeas corpus, the arrest and military trials of some "dissenters," the suppression of some Democratic and pro-southern newspapers, and the imposition of military drafts. But most of all it was the battlefield losses and stalled Union armies in 1864 that portended defeat for Lincoln and other Republicans. Seeing weakness in Lincoln or simply finding him insufficiently radical on matters of race and the proposed reconstruction of the South, some Republicans wanted to dump Lincoln for another candidate.[34]

As Matthew Pinsker shows in his chapter, Lincoln met the moment brilliantly because he was a seasoned and savvy politician. Lincoln deftly outmaneuvered his chief rival, Salmon P. Chase, and drew on his political friendships to gain support for his reelection. In the end, military success secured the victory. When William Tecumseh Sherman took Atlanta, Lincoln's stock rose. Lincoln also improved his fortunes within the party through his good relations with governors, local party leaders, and editors in key states, which made opposing him too costly a prospect for rivals. He managed his renomination with skill, and pulled the party together to back him, out of self-interest if not conviction. He then drew on his popularity among the soldiers and his unshakable commitment to winning the war to gain their vote, irrespective of their prior political leanings, which proved critical in several states. That Union soldiers were furloughed to vote and were allowed to vote in the field showed the administration's attention to the details of winning an election. Lincoln also benefited from the Democrats' call for an armistice and their nomination of General George McClellan as their presidential

Your Plan and Mine (New York, 1864), lithograph by Currier and Ives. This political cartoon loaded in the Republican themes of a resolute Lincoln willing to make no concessions to the "rebels" and standing firm with the black soldiers for freedom, while the Democratic presidential candidate George B. McClellan promises to give away the Union and submit to the ruthless slaveholders. Lincoln's image as a resolute commander in chief and political leader grew dramatically with his electoral success and the Union military gains in 1864. (Library of Congress)

candidate. Soldiers and many others saw in McClellan and the Democrats the likely selling out of the Union to the Confederacy, and Lincoln and the Republicans drove that point home. All this, as Pinsker argues, attests to Lincoln's leadership skills.

It is significant, too, that Lincoln never let the crisis corrupt or disrupt the regular election processes. The suppression of civil liberties notwithstanding, Lincoln never called for the postponement or end of elections or the banishment of the Democratic Party from elections. Lincoln's faith in democracy rested on his faith in the system of regularly scheduled elections, whereby parties had to be accountable and wherein the people might speak and act for their own interest.

As he stated in response to a serenade of his victory in November 1864, "The election was a necessity." He explained, "We can not have free government without elections; and if the rebellion could force us to forego, or postpone a national election, it might fairly claim to have already conquered and ruined us." The election, he noted, "demonstrated that a people's government can sustain a national election, in the midst of a great civil war," and thereby showed a doubting world the strength and resiliency of American democracy.[35] Thus Lincoln had taken his chances with the electorate. He thought he might lose the election in 1864 and told his cabinet to plan for an orderly transfer of power to the Democrats. He would accept the will of the people.

Even as Lincoln prepared for a possible defeat at the polls, he stayed focused on his principal responsibility as president—winning the war to save the Union and secure the "new birth of freedom." Lincoln reminded his cabinet that his administration would have to redouble its efforts to win the war before a McClellan administration would be sworn in. Such efforts would be the only way to bring the necessary victory for the Union and freedom that would surely be lost if the Democrats came to power. As the historian David Potter has observed, Lincoln's greatest contribution to the United States and the world was his respect for democratic processes. In the United States, nineteenth-century liberalism and nationalism converged and strengthened each other, thus assuring that the great experiment in self-government testified to the world that freedom need not be sacrificed for national unity. Such respect revealed Lincoln's greatest quality of leadership—political courage.[36]

Lincoln's genius in politics was not always matched by his genius as commander in chief. As Gregory Urwin reminds us in his chapter, historians disagree as to Lincoln's ability to understand and manage war. The consensus is that Lincoln became an effective, and even brilliant, commander in chief in terms of developing a strategic vision that marshaled the Union's military, political, and moral forces to sustain the war effort. But, some scholars argue, along the way he made mistakes that cost lives and lengthened the war. This was especially true in his inability to frame a military order in terms understandable to his generals, in his failure to develop a command system necessary to fight a "modern" war, and in his tendency to interfere too much. Early in the war, for example, he confused the military situation by issuing orders for a general advance and "borrowing" soldiers from General George McClellan to protect Washington, which had the counter-effect of adding to the ever-cautious McClellan's inclination to move slowly against the Confederate forces in Virginia. As Urwin shows, such criticisms carry weight. But, in the end, Lincoln proved more than equal to what he called the "great task remaining before us"—winning the war—by studying military history, manuals, maps, and soldiers and, most important, by being able to see the war for what it was, "a people's contest" that demanded drawing on all the resources of the Union to save it. His determination not to lose and his willingness to use all the instruments at hand, including self-important and politically ambitious generals, served the country well. The distinguished military historian T. Harry Williams once observed that in ranking generals, the true test of genius was easily determined: great generals win great victories. So, too, for Lincoln as commander in chief.[37]

On the face of it, Lincoln had little prospect for greatness as a commander in chief. He had no military experience, except for his brief time as a militia captain in the 1832 Black Hawk War when, by his account, the only actions he saw were "charges upon the wild onions" in the fields and the consequent "good many bloody struggles" with mosquitos.[38] But given the scale and character of the Civil War, it might fairly be argued that there were no relevant precedents for a commander in chief in such a war. In the two previous wars the nation fought after independence, President James Madison in the War of 1812 and President James Polk in the Mexican War left most military matters to the generals. The wars were short, the fighting largely far from the capital (though the British did burn Washington in the War of 1812), the communications with the armies slow and irregular, and the wars decided by diplomacy after hard fighting in the field.

The American Civil War, by contrast, was fought with large citizen-soldier armies and required the mobilization of the industrial, financial, agricultural, political, and psychological resources of a nation. Then, too, the Civil War was close at hand. Improved communications and transportation, especially the telegraph and railroads, had closed the distance between the home front and the battlefields. Armies tramped about in the land, bivouacked in towns across the country, and fought within earshot of the capital. Correspondents from newspapers followed the armies and brought their progress, or lack of it, home to the people, as they also built up expectations regarding military performance. And the Civil War could not end with a negotiated settlement that conceded the legitimacy of the Confederacy, for doing so would defeat the very reason for fighting for the Union at all. The war must be won or the great democratic republic would fail. Also, fighting a civil war demanded a different sensitivity than fighting a foreign foe, especially given the need to win the war in ways that would kill secession but not destroy the capacity to reunite the people. Lincoln understood all this and acted accordingly. In doing so, he defined the role of commander in chief.

Whatever his failings in particulars, Lincoln never lost sight of the grand objective—defeating the enemy armies. As he instructed his generals, the object was not to take the Confederate capital and engage in smart maneuvering that might bring the other side to the negotiating table; it was, rather, to put down a rebellion convincingly. That meant carrying the war to the enemy and destroying his capacity and will to resist. It meant action, lest the other side seize the initiative. What Lincoln proposed was a coordinated policy of naval blockade to deny the Rebels supplies and support, and aggressive military incursions across the line to force the enemy armies from the field. Lincoln understood that, properly managed, the Union had the manpower and material resources to press the Confederacy everywhere, making it impossible for it to defend all its interests and causing it to collapse.

Lincoln tried to convey his strategic design to his generals early on, but they either dismissed him as an uninformed bungler and meddler or ignored his advice as they worried about their particular theater of operation, almost irrespective of any grand strategy to win the war. Lincoln sought advice from his generals because he wanted to learn and know their interests. At the same time, he insisted on the importance of unified purpose and unitary command. The generals and the people must think in terms of consolidating and coordinating their strength to realize the common objective. In 1861 Lincoln explained to Congress, "It has been said that one bad general is better than two good ones; and the saying is true, if taken to mean no more than that an army is better directed by a single mind, though inferior, than by two superior ones, at variance, and cross purposes with each other." Thus, he continued, "the same is true, in all joint operations wherein those engaged, *can* have none but a common end in view, and *can* differ only as to the choice of means."[39]

In 1862 he summed up his strategic thinking in a letter to General Don Carlos Buell, who was "lost" in Tennessee and awaiting orders from his superior, General McClellan. Without interfering in McClellan's plans but wanting to push Buell to liberate unionist East Tennessee, Lincoln wrote:

> I state my general idea of this war to be that we have the *greater* numbers, and the enemy has the *greater* facility of concentrating forces upon points of collision; that we must fail, unless we can find some way of making *our*

advantage an over-match for *his*; and that this can only be done by menacing
him with superior forces at *different* points, at the *same* time; so that we can
safely attack, one, or both, if he makes no change; and if he *weakens* one to
strengthen the other, forbear to attack the strengthened one, but seize, and
hold the weakened one, gaining so much.[40]

That in essence was what became the Union strategy in practice after Lincoln
found generals, especially Ulysses S. Grant, who grasped its fundamental wisdom and acted on it.

Lincoln wanted action and was impatient with the petty jealousies and complaints of military men always begging for more time, more supplies, and more
men. In early 1862, for example, he sent a telegram to a balky Admiral Andrew
Hull Foote demanding that he provide naval support for General Ulysses S.
Grant's campaign against Forts Henry and Donelson in Tennessee. Lincoln asked
Foote to explain "What is lacking" and "What is being done so far as you know"
to dispatch the needed rafts and mortars. He ordered Foote to "Telegraph every
day, showing the progress, or lack of progress in this matter."[41]

As commander in chief, Lincoln understood that public opinion demanded
action, a fact he tried to relate to his generals, who, until the rise of Grant, Sherman, and Philip Sheridan, largely went unheeded. The generals would move at
their own pace and liking. Lincoln sought to move them faster. Thus, in April
1862—worried that the enemy was gaining the advantage in Virginia because
the Army of Potomac under General George McClellan was only inching its way
toward Richmond and the principal southern army in Virginia—Lincoln sent a
long letter to McClellan, wanting to know why McClellan was not pressing his
advantage of numbers and logistics. McClellan already had snubbed Lincoln and
cast himself as the savior of the Union, but Lincoln was not so much concerned
with McClellan's ego as with his will to fight. Lincoln dismissed McClellan's constant carping about needing more troops and support, writing, "Your despatches
complaining that you are not properly sustained, while they do not offend me, do
pain me very much." He proceeded to calculate the troop levels and concluded
that McClellan had enough to face the enemy. He warned McClellan that "by
delay the enemy will relatively gain upon you . . . faster by *fortifications* and *re-
inforcements*, than you can by re-inforcements alone." He insisted that McClellan
must "strike a blow." Lest McClellan resist the command, Lincoln leaked the letter to the press, which action also answered critics who thought Lincoln tolerated
McClellan's and other generals' lack of aggressiveness. Lincoln closed the letter

with a reassurance that he would "sustain you, so far as in my most anxious judgment, I consistently can," while observing that "the country will not fail to note—is now noting—that the present hesitation to move upon an intrenched enemy, is but the story of Manassas repeated."[42]

Lincoln's leadership was tested in his dealing with McClellan and similarly reluctant commanders. McClellan continued to exasperate Lincoln with his limited conception of the war, his complaints about lack of support, his intrigues, and, after the Battle of Antietam in September 1862, his reluctance to follow up a tactical victory by pursuing General Robert E. Lee's army in order to destroy it. In July 1862 Lincoln met with McClellan and generals on his staff to assess the situation in the field—one of eleven times Lincoln visited troops at the front. That visit encouraged the soldiers in the ranks, who came to admire Lincoln for his genuine concern for them,[43] but discouraged Lincoln, who came away doubting McClellan's ability to make an honest analysis of his advantages. Lincoln's detailed notes from his conversations reveal his interest in learning the facts for himself and taking the measure of the officers so that he might make intelligent decisions about needs and about whom to trust.

Already, Lincoln was pushing McClellan, and others, to use the abundant resources at hand to take on the enemy on all fronts. Lincoln sent barbed telegrams to McClellan to spur him on. On May 1, 1862, for example, he wrote, "Your call for Parrott guns from Washington alarms me—chiefly because it argues indefinite procrastination. Is anything to be done?" Most tellingly, in October 1862, Lincoln chided McClellan for his "over-cautiousness." He asked, "Are you not over-cautious when you assume that you can not do what the enemy is constantly doing? Should you not claim to be at least his equal in prowess, and act upon that claim?" He then instructed McClellan on war, urging him to "menace the enemies' communications," select the best route to Richmond, and fight the enemy army "if a favorable opportunity" came. Lincoln expected no less. "I say 'try,'" he wrote, for "if we never try, we shall never succeed." He concluded with an appeal to McClellan's honor: "It is all easy if our troops march as well as the enemy; and it is unmanly to say they can not do it."[44]

In this letter, Lincoln showed not only his impatience with McClellan but also his own growing self-confidence about how to conduct military operations. He did not order McClellan to follow any particular recommendations as to the line of march, but he expected McClellan to act forcefully. When McClellan continued to find excuses rather than push on against Lee's army after Antietam, Lincoln sacked him. He tried other generals, writing to each upon appointment about the need to keep the principal objectives always in mind and never to be afraid to fight. He also reminded them to deal honestly with the government and not to put their own interests ahead of the common good. Most telling, in January 1863 he admonished General Joseph Hooker, who had intrigued against his fellow officers and had criticized Lincoln's leadership, writing, "I have heard, in such a way as to believe it, of your recently saying that both the Army and the Government needed a Dictator. Of course it was not *for* this, but in spite of it, that I have given you the command [of the Army of the Potomac]. Only those generals who gain successes can set up dictators. What I now ask of you is military success, and I will risk the dictatorship." He continued, warning "Fighting Joe" Hooker that he "much" feared that "the spirit which you have aided to infuse into the Army, of criticizing their Commander, and withholding confidences from him, will now turn upon you," and promised to help Hooker "put it down." But, Lincoln observed, "neither you, nor Napoleon, if he were alive again, could get any good out of an army while such a spirit prevails in it." And he admonished Hooker: "Beware of rashness, but with energy, and sleepless vigilance, go forward, and give us victories."[45]

Victory did not come with Hooker, who was thrashed at the Battle of Chancellorsville in May 1863, and Lincoln turned to others. In doing so, he increasingly made his own assessments and discounted those whose judgments he had come to respect less. Lincoln became an excellent judge of talent and supported and promoted officers who showed intelligence, skill, and the will to fight, and who shared his strategic concepts. He also appreciated generals who used the resources at hand—in a word, those who fought much and wrote less. He stood by such men and no doubt gained satisfaction with their success. When several military men and Republicans wanted to sack General Ulysses S. Grant after the bloody Battle of Shiloh on April 6–7, 1862, because Grant had been caught with his guard down, Lincoln stood by Grant. Lincoln remarked that he had withstood the "stronger influence brought against Grant, praying for his removal, . . . than for any other object, coming too from good men," and noted that if he "had done as my Washington friends, who fight battles with their tongues instead of swords far from the enemy, demanded of me, Grant, who has proved himself so great a military captain, would never have been heard from again."[46] Lincoln recognized Grant's potential and encouraged it. He also investigated rumors about Grant's drinking and found them unwarranted or unrelated to Grant's generalship.

Lincoln's relationship with Grant in many ways revealed his maturing role as commander in chief. He supported Grant, but in 1863 he did not agree with the general's approach to taking Vicksburg and opening the vital Mississippi River to Union traffic. As a westerner, Lincoln appreciated the importance of the western theater to winning the war, and he watched developments there closely. He urged a more direct approach to taking Vicksburg, the last Confederate position blocking the river, but deferred to Grant's strategy of trying to divert the Mississippi, and failing that, then going around Vicksburg and fighting Confederate forces in detail before laying siege to the city. As public criticism of the lengthy campaign grew, Lincoln became anxious about Grant's plans and progress. But he did not interfere or cave in to critics wanting Grant dismissed. In the end, Grant's strategy succeeded. Lincoln admitted to Grant that he had been wrong to doubt Grant's approach—an act of humility and acknowledgment that reflected Lincoln's genius in dealing with men.[47]

After Vicksburg, Lincoln had found his man. By mid-1863, following the victories at Gettysburg and Vicksburg, Lincoln also began to turn over the management of the war to Secretary of War Edwin Stanton and General Henry Halleck, who served as army chief of staff. Also, with a more seasoned officer corps, Lincoln could trust generals in the field to make good assessments of needs and opportunities. He still had doubts about some generals' aggressiveness, including General George Gordon Meade because he failed to follow up his victory at Gettysburg with a vigorous pursuit of Lee's battered army (though Lincoln, not wanting to lose Meade or undermine his confidence, kept that frustration to himself and withheld a letter he wrote rebuking him). Lincoln continued to "interfere" by appointing or protecting political generals, which continued to frustrate commanders, and he still stressed the importance of making Lee's army, not Richmond, the primary objective in the East.[48] But Lincoln knew the war had turned decisively because of emancipation, and he "trusted" the new men, such as Grant, who had emerged to lead the way through fighting. The character of the war had changed. By 1863 hard war carried to civilians had become policy. That required new thinking and tough men.[49]

In 1864, once assured that Grant would not be a political challenger, Lincoln appointed him as commanding general of all the Union armies and brought him east, where Grant then made defeating Lee's army his principal interest. That emphasis well suited Lincoln, who, through Halleck, had made it clear to Grant that "All our forces in the east should be concentrated against Lee's army." Grant promised to move against the Confederates along a broad front and to hound the enemy every day. Lincoln much admired the plan and encouraged Grant to "chew & choke" with a bulldog grip on the enemy.[50] Such men as Lincoln now trusted finally defeated the Confederacy. In doing so, they also vindicated Lincoln's leadership as commander in chief.

Lincoln's leadership also derived from his ability to shape public opinion and to win people's trust in him—in effect, to explain and sustain the war effort through words. Lincoln never developed a systematic propaganda policy; rather, he wrote and spoke to meet particular needs. Lincoln understood that writing was an essential instrument of political, military, and moral leadership, and he worked hard to perfect his method and message.

Lincoln guarded his words, and also his image as it might derive from and inform what he said and wrote. As a prospective candidate for president, he had understood that public perceptions counted, and he tried to counter the image of him as an unsophisticated westerner by crafting careful speeches, such as his scholarly Cooper Union speech in New York City in February 1860 that documented and demonstrated both the dangers of the "slave power" and the need for Republicans to respect history and law and meet the moral obligation to stand against it. To be sure, the popular images of Lincoln as "the Rail-Splitter" and "Honest Abe" were political gold in a democracy that prized the self-made man, and in his days as a Whig politician and state legislator, he had played to the crowd with speeches mixed with logic, satire, homey phrases, and folk wisdom that made him popular on the stump. But Lincoln as president sought a more statesmanlike stance. He posed for photographs in ways intended to enhance his stature, giving him the appearance of gravity necessary for the presidential work he had to do. The mass production of such images on *cartes de visites* and in other publications insured their wide circulation. Similarly, Lincoln established an image as a father figure and family man—for example, the famous posed picture of him reading with his son Tad—that fit the popular mold for a trusted leader.[51]

Such images were in part due to the influence of Mary Todd Lincoln. Mrs. Lincoln was an astute political observer in her own right, and during Lincoln's days in Illinois she skillfully practiced parlor politics. As first lady, she sought to ensure her husband's favorable representation by advising him on appearance and other matters, and helped him seem more "presidential" in public settings. At the same time, however, her own excesses in spending on White House furnishings and social affairs worried Lincoln, who thought they would make him seem insensitive to the sufferings of the people. Likewise, her sometimes ill-timed efforts to secure appointments for family and favorites led to public criticism of her "intrusions." Mrs. Lincoln's Kentucky relations, which included pro-southern family

"Abraham Lincoln and His Son Tad Looking at an Album of Photographs," photograph by Anthony Berger, 1864. This image of Lincoln as family man was among the most popular Lincoln photographs of his day and was widely reproduced. In the original photograph, which is a rare instance of Lincoln shown wearing glasses, Lincoln and Tad are looking at a Mathew Brady album of photographs. In later issues the photograph was sometimes retouched, with the album replaced by a Bible. Such images added to Lincoln's reputation as "Father Abraham." (Library of Congress)

members wanting favors from the president, complicated Lincoln's public image. This was especially the case among abolitionists and Republicans who thought him too much beholden to the border states and slow to move against slavery. Perceptions mattered.[52]

For Lincoln, controlling his image meant controlling both the contexts and the texts. He did not want to be misunderstood or misrepresented. Thus, in standing before the public, Lincoln as president shifted to speaking from prepared texts, which he had drafted carefully, with much forethought and frequent revision before settling on a final version. Even during the exultation over the fall of Richmond in April 1865, Lincoln addressed a celebrating crowd that had gathered outside the White House by reading, with candlelight, from a "carefully prepared manuscript."[53]

Lincoln loved the magic and power of words and worked at his craft. As he wrote in a lecture on "discoveries and inventions" in 1859, "*Writing*—the art of communicating thoughts to the mind, through the eye—is the great invention of the world." Writing was the means by which thought became analysis and human improvement became possible.[54]

Lincoln did so not only in drafting papers, letters, and speeches for public audiences, but also in composing memos to himself to sort out his own thinking. This was especially the case as he pondered the deeper meaning of the war and worked through his own understanding of the place of the United States in God's plan and in history. As the war progressed, Lincoln searched for God's purpose and concluded as early as 1862 that God's way of accomplishing His purposes might not be hitched to the Union's military fortunes. In the fall of 1862, he wrote a meditation on the war to make sense of it. His meditation was for and to himself—an example of Lincoln's habit of working out ideas on paper. In the text, Lincoln wrote, "The will of God prevails. In great contests each party claims to act in accordance with the will of God. Both *may* be, and one *must* be wrong. God can not be *for*, and *against* the same thing at the same time." From this, Lincoln concluded that "In the present civil war it is quite possible that God's purpose is something different from the purposes of either party. . . . I am almost ready to say this is probably true—that God wills this contest, and wills that it shall not end yet."[55] This meditation revealed Lincoln's process of analyzing a problem, recalling his lawyerly method of weighing all possibilities. It also pointed to Lincoln's rapidly evolving religious thinking that the war was a price the nation must pay for its sin of slavery.[56] As Harry S. Stout shows in his chapter, Lincoln's religious journey, worked out in his writing, became an important part of Lincoln's understanding of why the war came, why it exacted such a large blood sacrifice, and why it mattered. All this was related in his Second Inaugural Address in March 1865, which, after his death, became Lincoln's benediction to the nation.

Lincoln drew on many sources in his thinking and writing. He had a particular affinity for Shakespeare, Scripture, and the Scottish poet Robert Burns. His self-education growing up also included Enlightenment writers, whose thought informed and reinforced his own personal preference for achieving balance and prizing self-control. And he read many speeches. He especially admired those of Henry Clay, the great Whig legislator who was one of Lincoln's heroes for his "American System," love of the Union, and commonsense approaches to problems. At the same time, Lincoln enjoyed tall tales, fables, and storytelling, all of which gave him a stock of yarns to spin by the stove in country stores while riding the circuit as a lawyer in Illinois or stumping for candidates. He later used them in the White House while making his case or deflecting all manner of congressmen, cabinet officers, generals, clergy, office seekers, and others wanting favors or demanding some action from the beleaguered president. As a lawyer and prairie state politician, Lincoln also learned to listen to the common speech of the people, and he became attuned to its rhythms and folk wisdom. The sources were thus myriad and many. Lincoln used and mixed them as fit the need and the audience.[57]

Lincoln read copiously during his presidency. He was almost unique among nineteenth-century presidents after John Quincy Adams in doing so. He continued especially to read Shakespeare (mostly the tragedies), the Bible, and poetry. All no doubt provided welcome relief from battle reports, casualty lists, political sheets, and other daily fare that came across his desk. He also read military manuals and history to learn the art and manner of war. He studied human nature. He read to learn and thus to lead.

Lincoln's writings and speeches echoed the sources in content and cadences, but they all had Lincoln's own stamp. Throughout his writing ran an emphasis on reason over passion, respect for law, moral purpose, the strength of democratic institutions, trust in the common sense of the people, and, as the war progressed, God's providential hand shaping the history of what Lincoln once referred to as the "almost chosen people." Throughout, it also was an honest empathy for the sufferings and losses of others. He wrote and spoke in terms of the collective "we the people" rather than projecting himself as the focus of public concerns. The style, like the man, was lean and tough and free of the artifice so common among political figures of his day.

During his presidency, Lincoln made few speeches, and rarely gave extemporaneous ones. He wanted his words to be clear and to carry weight when he did speak or write for public consumption. The issues were too important to risk misunderstandings, and the politics too charged to invite distortions. Also, Lincoln feared overusing the power of what Teddy Roosevelt later called the "bully pulpit" of the presidency. Words worked best when tied to action. They also prepared the ground for policy, as in his careful public statements regarding the necessity of accepting emancipation as essential for winning the war. Thus, as Stout and others have argued, Lincoln's public addresses command special attention for their care, conviction, and circumstance. And as Stout especially observes, they need to be read also for Lincoln's efforts to understand and appeal to the conscience of the people.

Lincoln's writings and speeches not only explained interests and policy, but also inspired people to consider their interest and to fight for it. In his major public addresses, he wrote for posterity as much as for the present circumstance. Doing so, as Harry S. Stout insists, gave Lincoln's ideas and policies a compelling force in his day and enduring meaning for generations thereafter. The power of Lincoln's words came especially from what the historian David Potter described as Lincoln's cosmic vision of the Union's—the nation's—place in history and human progress. Their power came, too, from the common awareness that Lincoln believed in what he said and acted on it. Therein lay much of the force of his leadership.

For a man who never traveled outside the United States, Lincoln had a profound sense of the nation's place in the world. His experience as a surveyor, shopkeeper, legislator, and lawyer and his travels campaigning across much of the Old Northwest and later in the East had introduced him to a wide compass of American interests, ideas, and institutions. From such travels in the United States, he gained faith in the people and the country. All this made him keenly aware of the need to work at making the democratic experiment succeed. Such belief infused his public addresses. Lincoln summed up cause and consequence for all time in his Gettysburg Address, which called on Americans to fulfill the promise and obligations of the American Revolution. He did so with biblical cadences and language that magnified the message beyond the moment. With "increased devotion," Lincoln avowed, Americans must honor the living and the dead by continuing "the great task remaining before us . . . that this nation, under God, shall have a new birth of freedom—and that government of the people, by the people, for the people, shall not perish from the earth."[58]

Behold Oh! America, Your Sons! The Greatest Among Men (Chicago, 1865), lithograph by Louis Kurz, published by Charles Shober. The image of Lincoln and Washington as maker and savior of the nation became a common trope in imagery and history. This image reflected a popular theme in Lincoln lore that Lincoln was the true heir of what Washington and the Founding Fathers had built. Lincoln as "Savior of the Union" equaled his legacy as the "Great Emancipator" in the popular mind thereafter. (Library of Congress)

But it took more than words to win what Lincoln termed "a people's contest." It took hard fighting, hard politics, and hard truths. In the end, the measure of Lincoln's leadership was decided by success in arms, the ability of Lincoln and his party to hold and use power to effect their basic interests, and his capacity to put the war and emancipation in proper perspective.

On those matters, no consensus exists among historians as to the genius of Lincoln's leadership. And on these questions, in this book, the historians Gregory Urwin, Matthew Pinsker, Harry Stout, and Allen Guelzo suggest there is more to Lincoln's practice as commander in chief, head of his party, and spokesman for the conscience and cause of the nation than the abundant histories and biographies of the times and the man have fully realized. And, as much as we know about Lincoln, there is much left to know. Thus the contributions to this book. In them, the authors point to particulars in Lincoln's decision making and relations with others, in uniform and in his party especially, that warrant attention. If, as David Donald and others have argued, the Lincoln story will always be unfinished because of Lincoln's "essential ambiguity" and the complexities of the age, it invites such new, and nuanced, perspectives that each contributor offers on Lincoln and war, Lincoln and politics, and Lincoln and the soul of the people.

At Lincoln's deathbed, a distraught Edwin Stanton supposedly observed that "now he [Lincoln] belongs to the ages."[59] The apotheosis of Lincoln began almost immediately upon his death. Paintings, poetry, and all manner of public speeches, histories, memorials, and more, lifted Lincoln to the bosom of God in the public imagination and memory. His sanctification made him almost unreachable and unknowable, and thus even unbelievable. Debunkers and critics at different times have tried to pull him down from the pedestals his legions of admirers built for him, especially lately on matters of race, and serious scholars have placed him in historical context and tried to understand the man and his appeal. Doing so has humanized Lincoln and in many ways made him more "relevant" because more believable. In such investigations, scholars discovered an imperfect man, and leader, able to grow and willing to do so. This recognition worked especially to enhance appreciation of Lincoln's leadership. As such, Lincoln belongs not only to the ages, or the angels, but also to each generation needing to consider the character and consequence of the man who, more than any other, has come to embody "America" here and across the world. It answers the question that echoes from the bicentennial of Lincoln's birth in 2009—namely, why Lincoln matters.

2

Sowing the Wind and Reaping the Whirlwind

Abraham Lincoln as a War President

Gregory J. W. Urwin

Any consideration of Abraham Lincoln as a war president must attempt to contrast image with historical reality. When it comes to Lincoln, of course, there is no shortage of images. Our conception of this fascinating, contradictory man has been shaped by a mountain of books and articles, as well as numerous works from photographers, painters, sculptors, poets, playwrights, and screenwriters.[1]

Perhaps the most appropriate way to start wrestling with this titanic figure is to consider the way that Union veterans—the men Lincoln considered his chief partners in the struggle to preserve the American experiment in federated self-government—viewed their commander in chief.[2] On July 4, 1894, Cuyahoga County, Ohio, dedicated its Soldiers' and Sailors' Monument, a $280,000 tribute in stone and bronze, on Cleveland's spacious Public Square. Designed by Levi T. Scofield, a former Union Army captain turned architect, the monument featured a fifteen-foot statue of an armed Goddess of Liberty towering over the Cleveland skyline from a shaft more than one hundred feet tall.

Scofield guarded the approaches to the Soldiers' and Sailors' Monument with four larger-than-life groups of statuary, which he sculpted himself. These represented the contributions of the Union's four combat arms, the Infantry, Cavalry, Artillery, and Navy. Inside the ornately carved granite and Amherst stone building encasing the shaft's base, Scofield placed four bronze bas-reliefs commemorating pivotal moments in the war. Scofield chose the entrance from Superior Avenue as the setting for the most dramatic of these scenes, "The Emancipation of the Slave."

Standing in the forefront of this tableau is Scofield's vision of Lincoln the war president. What we see here is not the gentle "Father Abraham" of beloved memory, but a virile, militant man striking a pose of righteous defiance. Portrayed in full relief, he seems to be lunging from the bronze panel. Backed by four of Ohio's prominent wartime politicians (Salmon P. Chase, John Sherman, Benjamin Wade, and Joshua R. Giddings) and the serried ranks of the Union Army and Navy, Lincoln brandishes the broken shackles of slavery in his upraised right hand and extends a soldier's rifle musket and accoutrements to a muscular African American—who kneels in gratitude for his freedom but proudly holds his head upraised as he takes the oath of enlistment.[3]

This is Lincoln as the boys in blue remembered him—strong, decisive, and willing to shake the foundations of the nation's social order to ensure the preservation of the republic and "a new birth of freedom."

Recent surveys reveal that most American historians continue to rate Abraham Lincoln as this country's best president. This subjective judgment hinges primarily on Lincoln's performance as commander in chief in the Civil War, in which he surmounted a host of daunting challenges and succeeded in both preserving the Union and destroying slavery. Lincoln turned out to be more than a successful wartime chief executive. His actions defined the presidency's role in the American way of war, setting precedents that affected the conduct of his successors down to our own time.

Professor T. Harry Williams of Louisiana State University, a leading Civil War historian of the 1950s and 1960s, identified the qualities that made Lincoln such an effective commander in chief by quoting Carl von Clausewitz, the Prussian military theorist. That astute veteran of the Napoleonic Wars, whose ideas were unknown to Americans of Lincoln's day, argued that "a remarkable, superior mind and strength of character" mattered more in a war leader than did extensive military experience.[4]

The conventional view of Lincoln as a war leader, which Professor Williams did so much to nurture, casts the melancholy Illinoisan as an untutored genius. He needed to be a genius, as his résumé for directing the largest armed conflict that his country had yet known was sadly deficient. Lincoln's only direct knowledge of soldiering came from a short turn as a militia captain in the Black Hawk War. He saw no combat, except for what he jokingly characterized as "a good many bloody struggles with the mosquitoes," and he fell far short of distinguishing himself as an officer. Although an able lawyer and a masterful politician, Lincoln lacked the executive experience deemed necessary to lead a nation through a trial as harrowing as the Civil War.[5]

Nevertheless, Lincoln possessed an array of traits and talents that made him equal to his terrible task. A highly intelligent man, he had a knack for cutting through superfluous detail to grasp the essence of complex issues and problems. He also benefited from clarity of vision and steel-hard resolution. He knew exactly what he wanted to accomplish with his war—save the Union. Every other consideration took second place to that. Lincoln's obsession with preventing the balkanization of the United States rested on his conception of what his nation represented. He believed that the American republic not only served the best interests of its own people, but also offered a beacon of hope to the rest of humanity.[6] This is what Lincoln meant when he said, "This is essentially a People's contest. On the side of the Union it is a struggle for maintaining in the world, that form, and substance of government, whose leading object is, to elevate the condition of men—to lift artificial weights from all shoulders—to clear the paths of laudable pursuit for all—to afford all, an unfettered start, and a fair chance, in the race of life."[7] This almost mystical vision of America's mission to lead the human race to a freer form of existence is why Lincoln called his cause "the last best hope of earth"—humanity's only chance to avoid a future cursed by tyranny and darkness.[8]

And because the Union's preservation meant so much to so many, Lincoln was willing to do whatever it took to accomplish that objective. Beginning with a moderate military policy that attempted to subdue the Confederacy without touching slavery, Lincoln would steadily escalate the war by endorsing harsher measures championed by the Radical Republicans and putting his own twist on them—property confiscation, slave emancipation, and finally the widespread destruction of both public and private resources in the rebellious states.[9]

Lincoln also decided that the demands of national security occasionally justified the curtailment of civil liberties. The president boldly suspended the writ of habeas corpus, subjecting citizens that he and his subordinates deemed disloyal to arrest without warrant and to trial by military tribunals. The Lincoln administration went so far as to temporarily close down hostile newspapers or refuse others the right to mail issues to subscribers. Lincoln's critics denounced him as a despot in language much more violent than that aimed at George W. Bush after the passage of the Patriot Act and the establishment of a detention center for suspected terrorists at Guantanamo Bay. In an incredible coincidence, a British protest in the summer of 1864 revealed that some of these political prisoners were subjected to a painful form of water torture, a practice that the White House did not attempt to curtail. Lincoln even acquiesced in the persecution of his most virulent congressional critic, Representative Clement L. Vallandigham of Ohio, who was tried for treason and exiled to the Confederacy.[10]

Yet for all these extreme examples, Lincoln did not wield his inferred powers as commander in chief in an arbitrary fashion. Mark E. Neely Jr. won a Pulitzer

Bombardment of Fort Sumter, Charleston Harbor, 12th and 13th of April 1861 (New York, 1861), lithograph by Currier and Ives. This popular print bespoke Union patriotism in depicting the American flag flying defiantly against the Confederacy's bombardment. News of the Confederate attack on Fort Sumter galvanized north-ern public opinion for strong measures to put down the rebellion, and Lincoln called up seventy-five thousand militia to do so. Lincoln acted without waiting for congressional endorsement, thus early on in the war showing his willingness to assume responsibility to act under his authority as commander in chief. (Library of Congress)

Prize in 1992 for his book *The Fate of Liberty: Abraham Lincoln and Civil Liber-ties*, which determined that the Union government made most of its military arrests in those areas that could be considered militarily sensitive—the border states and conquered stretches of the Confederacy.[11] Nevertheless, Lincoln came close to arguing that the ends justify the means when he inserted this appeal defending the suppression of dissidents in his famous message to Congress on July 4, 1861: "Are all the laws, *but one*, to go unexecuted, and the government itself go to pieces, lest that one be violated?"[12] Because Lincoln said it—and said it 150 years ago—it does not sound as unsettling as it would coming from a more recent occupant of the White House, but those chilling words testify to how far the sixteenth president would go to win his war. No one knew that better than did Robert Garlick Hill Kean, an official in the Confederate War Department, who vented in his diary on August 26, 1863, "All the revolutionary vigor is with the enemy, in legislation and execution. With us timidity, hair-splitting, and an absence of all *policy*."[13]

Lincoln stretched the Constitution and international law in other ways when he felt the circumstances warranted. During the war's first month, he ordered the expansion of the Union Navy and regular army, and also the enlistment of long-term volunteer troops, all without the authorization of Congress. He proclaimed the implementation of a naval blockade along the Confederate coast even though such a tactic normally required a declaration of war. Lincoln never requested such a mandate, as that would have implied recognition of the Confederacy as a separate nation—a principle Lincoln refused to concede. He remained adamant that he was quelling an insurrection and not suppressing a legitimate bid for southern independence. That was why the official Union name for this conflict was the War of the Rebellion.[14]

As T. Harry Williams and other historians see it, Lincoln demonstrated a similar perspicacity in his conduct of military affairs. They credit him with a greater appreciation for overall strategy than many of his generals. Lincoln decided early on that victory depended on the destruction of Confederate armies and not just the occupation of territory. Likewise, he realized that the best way to utilize the North's numerical superiority was to have Union field armies cooperate by launching coordinated offensives against the entire enemy perimeter. That would prevent the outnumbered Rebels from shifting reserves to threatened sectors, and thereby hasten their collapse.[15] "I state," he wrote to two of his generals in early 1862, "my general idea of the war to be that we have the greater numbers, and the enemy has the greater facility of concentrating forces upon points of collision; that we must fail unless we can find some way of making an advantage of overmatch for his; and this can be done only by menacing him with superior forces at different points at the same time."[16]

Lincoln also receives credit for giving the Union military a unified command system—even though it took him more than half the war to identify the senior commanders who would make it work effectively. Lincoln facilitated that development by acquiring the confidence and judgment to relieve incompetent or mediocre generals and replace them with commanders imbued with the energy, imagination, and killer instinct necessary to win America's bloodiest war. Once

"President Lincoln and Genl. Scott Reviewing 3 Years Regiment on Penn Ave.
1861," pencil and Chinese white drawing on green paper by Alfred R. Waud, 1861.
Lincoln turned to General Winfield Scott in the first months of the war to develop
military strategy. Scott proposed a naval blockade and a slow but steady process of
strangling the seceded states, but Lincoln wanted a faster, surer strategy because he
did not think the Union could stand a drawn-out war. The Union defeat at Manassas further convinced Lincoln and military men that the war would take great
effort. Lincoln called for longer enlistments and sought to rally public support with
the promise of military vigor. (Library of Congress)

Lincoln handed the reins of high command to Lieutenant General Ulysses S.
Grant, another unpretentious westerner who saw the war as he did, he could
stand back and let the Union Army and Navy do their job.[17]

That is the familiar view of how Lincoln ran the Civil War—a formula repeated
countless times and in a wide variety of formats. Like so many other aspects of
the Civil War, Lincoln's role has been lacquered with a veneer of sentimentality
and wrapped in a sense of inevitability that prevent us from appreciating just how

horrible that conflict was—and what sort of man it took to win it. The fact that the United States became one of the world's richest and most productive nations in the generation following Appomattox inclines Americans to regard the Civil War simply as a slight detour in the republic's irrepressible rise to greatness.[18] They forget that republics have been an anomaly for most of human history and that this country came perilously close between 1861 and 1865 to joining history's long list of failed democracies. Somehow, Americans regard the four years of ferocious mass murder that pinned the Union back together as the expression of something noble in the American character—rather than a manifest tragedy that unleashed baser impulses. Lincoln fits in this romanticized picture as kind old Father Abraham, whose soaring rhetoric and advocacy for a conciliatory peace settlement converted the war into a purging process that made the United States better as well as stronger.

This tendency to reduce history to an inspiring pageant helps foster a sense of national pride and identity, but it deprives us of some of the most important lessons that the past has to teach us. In particular, this larger-than-life Lincoln— part prophet, part secular saint—robs the man of his humanity and impedes the ability of this generation of embattled Americans to relate to him and profit properly from his example.

Lincoln himself is partly responsible for our clouded perception. Like other public figures, he donned masks that suited certain circumstances, and those masks still keep us from getting to know the inner man. A good example of such obfuscation is this seemingly typical example of Lincolnesque humility: "I claim not to have controlled events, but confess plainly that events have controlled me."[19] While there is much truth in that statement, it would be a mistake to think that fate alone turned Abraham Lincoln into a war president. He chose that role for himself through a series of calculated decisions fraught with peril. Unable to believe that most white southerners actually wished to turn their backs on their common heritage with the North, Lincoln rejected efforts to resolve the secession crisis through compromise. The newly inaugurated president risked armed conflict by refusing to evacuate Fort Sumter, the Federal island fortress that sat in full view of Charleston, South Carolina, the secessionist seedbed and most militant city in the newborn Confederacy. After Confederate gunners bombarded Sumter and forced the removal of its garrison, Lincoln embraced a military solution by summoning seventy-five thousand militiamen to suppress the southern rebellion.[20]

In the weeks before Lincoln took office, he dismissed pleas for a compromise solution by telling Republican senators, "The tug has to come, & better now, than any time hereafter."[21] He may have been right. Most historians believe that Fort Sumter had assumed such symbolic importance in the unionist camp that its seizure demanded Lincoln meet force with force or appear impotent. On the other hand, it could be argued that precipitating hostilities over a battle that cost no human lives was an overreaction, and Lincoln might have gained more by continuing to play a waiting game. Regardless of this question of timing, we should not forget that this cunning and often ruthless man ended up committing himself and his countrymen to paying an exceedingly heavy price in both blood and treasure to save the Union he so revered. In achieving that goal, he adopted war policies that visited catastrophic repercussions on both friend and foe. Lincoln could not foresee how destructive the Civil War was going to be, and the heat of that inferno seared his soul as much as any other American who experienced it. Nevertheless, he dragged the republic through the valley of the shadow because he could conceive of no other way to keep it whole. Abraham Lincoln wrote his name across the pivotal period of American history in letters of fire that consumed the lives of 620,000 soldiers in blue and gray. In the spirit of Shakespearean drama, the conflagration that Lincoln helped light in the end claimed him among its final victims.[22]

One of the prevailing themes in the literature on the Civil War Lincoln is how much he grew in office. When it came to military affairs, however, historians often gloss over how much growing this shrewd country lawyer needed to do. Lincoln made mistakes—big mistakes—even after he had years of experience under his belt.[23]

Lincoln's faults were especially evident in the months leading up to war and in the struggle's first year. He consistently underestimated the commitment of the seven states of the Lower South to the Confederacy they formed in February 1861. He thought if he followed a passive course and played for time, white southerners would calm down and return to the Union, which is another reason why he refused to consider calls for concessions to secessionists. Lincoln finally took aggressive action after the attack on Fort Sumter by mobilizing seventy-five thousand militia. He may have hoped that gesture would have had an intimidating effect on the secessionists. It did not. In fact, it made matters infinitely worse by prompting Virginia, Tennessee, North Carolina, and Arkansas to join the Confederacy. This development greatly prolonged the war, as these four states would furnish more than 40 percent of the Confederacy's soldiers, more than 50 percent of its industrial capacity, half of its food crops, and close to half of its horses and mules.[24]

The idea that Lincoln steadily became a better judge of military talent as the war went on, and that he filled the Union high command with superior officers, is also open to question. True, he had enough sense to elevate Ulysses S. Grant to the rank of lieutenant general and appointed him General in Chief of the Armies of the United States in mid-March 1864, but he still hobbled Grant with a coterie of highly placed political generals who had repeatedly demonstrated their military limitations for the past three years. As the campaign season opened that spring, Major General Nathaniel P. Banks, the former Speaker of the House of Representatives, commanded the Department of the Gulf with headquarters at New Orleans. Based out of Fort Monroe, Virginia, Major General Benjamin F. Butler, a one-time Democratic congressman from Massachusetts, was supposed to cooperate with Grant's offensive against Richmond by advancing on the Rebel capital from the east with the Army of the James. The erratic and temperamental Major General Franz Sigel, the darling of the North's German American community, stood poised to hand the Confederates yet another victory in the Shenandoah Valley as commander of the Department of West Virginia.[25]

This lackluster threesome did not hold token backwater commands. Lincoln gave them control of major field armies, which magnified their inadequacies into serious threats to the health of the Union cause. Sigel's blunders, for instance, permitted the Confederates to utilize once again the Shenandoah Valley as an invasion corridor. Hoping to reduce Union pressure on Richmond and Petersburg, Virginia, Lieutenant General Jubal A. Early marched down the valley and alarmed the Yankee home front by menacing the outskirts of Washington with fourteen thousand gray-clad troops on July 11.[26]

Far from giving Grant a free hand in the formulation and execution of strategy, Lincoln intervened from the start and compromised the cordon approach that he had supposedly championed from the early days of the conflict. Grant wanted Banks to capture Mobile, Alabama, and deprive the Confederacy of its last major port on the Gulf of Mexico, which would greatly tighten the Union naval blockade and further starve the enemy's war machine. Lincoln, however, approved a harebrained scheme proposed by Nathaniel Banks to invade Texas via Louisiana's Red River. Not only was Banks's Red River Expedition an unwarranted diversion that detracted from Grant's coherent strategy, but the evidence indicates that it was motivated more by a desire to obtain new cotton supplies for northern speculators than the illusory hope that it could reclaim Texas for the Union. Banks aborted his expedition after suffering two embarrassing defeats at the hands of a numerically inferior Confederate army, and came uncomfortably close to los-

ing the naval component of his combined force when water levels dropped on
the Red River. A more competent Union general would move against Mobile in
March 1865, and the city fell on April 12—three days after General Robert E. Lee's
surrender at Appomattox and two days before Lincoln's assassination.[27]

Although Grant must have resented Lincoln's meddling, he had the good
sense not to show it, which accounts in large part for why he and the president
got along as well as they did. The same could not be said for the vain perfection-
ist Major General George Brinton McClellan, the architect and first commander
of the Army of the Potomac, the Union's largest field army, and also Lincoln's
general in chief from November 1, 1861, to March 11, 1862. The disrespect that
"Little Mac" exhibited toward his commander in chief has not helped his historical reputation among generation after generation of Americans steeped in
Lincoln worship. McClellan was clearly less of an asset to the Union cause than
was Lincoln, but his conduct did not stem entirely from haughty self-assurance.
One of the reasons McClellan did not confide in Lincoln on military matters
was that he believed politicians were blabbermouths. While Lincoln was much
more circumspect than McClellan realized, other members of the administration
justified the general's apprehensions. This made a working relationship between
McClellan and Lincoln close to impossible. The wonder is that Lincoln stood the
situation as long as he did.[28]

Other regular army officers viewed Lincoln with similar contempt, and history has not dealt kindly with them either. It needs to be stated, however, that
Lincoln never achieved sufficient understanding of the cultural ethos that produced the U.S. Army's professional officer corps. These men believed that officers
were made, not born. The War of 1812 taught Winfield Scott and other gentlemen
who decided to commit their lives to the profession of arms that the nation's security depended on maintaining a hardened cadre of seasoned professional soldiers. Those admitted to this indispensable fraternity would have to pass through
years of rigorous education and training within the monastic confines of the U.S.
Military Academy, followed by more years of practical experience through war
and peace.[29] Officers who withstood the purging regimen at West Point resented
politicians who failed to respect their expertise and pulled strings to award commissions to influential constituents with no military background. On July 16,
1838, Cadet Henry Wager Halleck complained, "It is hard for us to be placed under citizens who have spent no time in preparation for their commissions, while
we have spent four or five years here at hard toil fitting ourselves for the various
duties of our stations."[30]

"Antietam, Md. President Lincoln with Gen. George B. McClellan and Group of Officers, October 3, 1862," photograph by Alexander Gardner, 1862. Lincoln urged his generals to make attacking the Confederate armies the principal strategy, rather than capturing the capital and occupying territory. He was unable to communicate his strategy effectively in military terms, however, and suffered from generals such as McClellan who did not trust him with their military planning, sought a more limited war than Lincoln wanted, and moved too cautiously to hammer the enemy. Lincoln's inability to understand the military mind earned him criticism and even snubs from many generals. Lincoln visited them in the field to discover their thinking and push their effort, but he did not tolerate failure to fight aggressively. He sacked McClellan for his "case of the slows" in not dogging Lee's retreating army after the battle of Antietam. (Library of Congress)

It was bad enough that Lincoln doled out a significant number of generals' appointments to politicians who were as ignorant of soldiering as he was. What really rankled the republic's professional soldiers was having Lincoln second-guessing them, altering their plans, and pressing them to attack before they were sure of victory. As a boy captain, George Armstrong Custer served on McClellan's staff, and he imbibed his chief's truculent attitude toward the president. In the serialized Civil War memoirs that Custer published in the months preceding his death at the Little Bighorn on June 25, 1876, he let those feelings resurface. While commenting on an order Lincoln issued on January 27, 1862, directing "a general movement of the land and naval forces of the United States against the insurgent forces," Custer observed, "This order cannot be classed among the many wise productions from the pen of President Lincoln. It was what might be expected, however, from an unmilitary man anxious and zealous to perform a military act, forgetting that it required in its inception and execution the highest professional ability and training known to the profession of arms." In other words, most professional soldiers thought Lincoln was no more qualified to tell them how to do their duty than he was to perform surgery.[31]

Ironically, it was the indignant Cadet Halleck who turned into the man who later enabled Lincoln to bridge this gap. The closest thing that passed for a military intellectual in the antebellum army, Halleck filled a staff assignment in California after its conquest by American forces in early 1847. Jettisoning the professional soldier's code of noninvolvement in civilian politics, he became a delegate to the convention that drafted California's state convention. While still retaining his military commission, Halleck served as California's secretary of state, joined a San Francisco law firm, and became a leading force in urban development. After resigning from the army on August 1, 1854, Halleck went into business and earned a fortune. He also became a noted authority on land-title issues and international law. Halleck donned a uniform once more with the outbreak of the Civil War, and soon received command of Union troops in the West. Lincoln named him general in chief in July 1862. Content to act as a coordinator and administrator, Halleck did not turn out to be the decisive supreme commander that the president desired. Yet because Halleck understood both the military mind and the civilian world, he became an effective communications conduit, helping Union generals to understand and accept Lincoln's directives. At the same time, he interpreted military jargon and explained the assumptions of the Union brass to the commander in chief. When Grant succeeded Halleck as general in chief in March 1864, the latter continued to play this vital role by staying on as his new superior's chief of staff. Thanks to this three-way partnership forged by Lincoln, Halleck, and Grant, the republic and its army arrived at a healthier relationship and persevered to win a huge and terrible war.[32]

Success in war is usually purchased by sacrificing human lives—both those of the enemy and your own people. This is true even when a president or his military commanders make the right decisions. Leaders who recoil from this formula—or who hesitate to embrace it—often end up presiding over defeats. Lincoln acquired a facility for making hard decisions just when they would deliver the most impact. Although his increasingly radical policies exacerbated the Confederacy's distress, they also unleashed forces that Lincoln could not always control. His most inspired and extreme move, the Emancipation Proclamation, propelled a nation torn by a war that had already set records in bloodletting and cash expenditures into a social revolution of unprecedented scale.[33] Lincoln combined this blow against slavery with an invitation to African Americans to join the Union Army as soldiers. That turned out to be an equally fateful step that caused the conflict to sink to new levels of savagery.

When Lincoln offered blacks a chance to fight for the Union, he also gave them the opportunity to carve a new place for themselves in the country's postwar social and political order. That was the vision that inspired many men of color to enlist. As an anonymous member of the 54th Massachusetts Volunteer Infantry Regiment wrote to a black religious newspaper, "If we understand the Declaration of Independence, it asserts the freedom and equality of all men. We ask nothing more. Give us equality and acknowledge us as men, and we are willing to stand by the flag of our Union and support the leaders of this great Government until every traitor shall be banished from our shore."[34] Lincoln would vindicate those hopes by citing black military service as his reason for refusing to publicly distance himself from emancipation even after it appeared to become a political liability during his 1864 reelection campaign. He also hinted toward the end of his life that black veterans should be allowed to vote.[35]

By accepting men of color as soldiers, however, Lincoln touched the white South on the raw nerve of its most dreaded fear—the threat of race war and servile insurrection. That, in turn, made the Union's black defenders the objects of hatred and the targets of numerous atrocities. To understand the backlash elicited by the creation of the U.S. Colored Troops, we must examine the values and anxieties that drove the South to secede in the first place.[36]

A major reason why Confederates fought so fiercely to defend slavery is that they could not conceive of it being ended peacefully. The rationale justifying human bondage held not only that blacks were inferior to people of European descent, but also that they were inherently savage and would turn on the white population if they were ever freed. This was what Thomas Jefferson meant when he confided sadly to a friend on April 22, 1820, "But as it is, we have the wolf by the ear, and we can neither hold him, nor safely let him go. Justice is in one scale,

Freedom to the Slave (np, 1863?), colored lithograph. The Emancipation Proclamation included the call for the enlistment of blacks as soldiers. Manpower needs dictated such a move, but so too did arguments from abolitionists that freedom required letting blacks fight for the cause and thereby earning their place as citizens. Recruiting posters and rallies emphasized such themes. On the reverse of this lithograph, showing what the progress of arms promised, was a recruiting poster that read, "All slaves were made Freemen. By Abraham Lincoln, President of the United States, January 1st, 1863. Come, then, able-bodied Colored Men, to the nearest United States Camp, and fight for the Stars and Stripes." (Library Company of Philadelphia)

and self-preservation in the other." Jefferson expressed the same thoughts more succinctly four years later: "We have the wolf by the ears and feel the danger of either holding or letting him loose." For as much as slavery troubled the author of the Declaration of Independence, he could not see a safe way for the South to release the wolf. The bloody excesses that attended the Haitian Revolution of 1792 and Nat Turner's revolt in Virginia in 1831 convinced white southerners—including non-slaveholders—that loss of control over the slave population would result in a merciless race war that would end in the extermination of either the South's whites or its blacks.[37]

These assumptions go a long way toward explaining the outrage voiced by white southerners in response to the militant abolitionist movement that arose in the North in the 1830s. Radicals like William Lloyd Garrison posed a threat not only to the South's pride and moral, economic, and political standing, but also to its white population's personal safety. That was why Virginia Congressman Henry A. Wise (a future Confederate general) denounced mounting abolitionist agitation in 1835 with these words: "Sir, slavery is interwoven with our very political existence, is guaranteed by our Constitution, and its consequences must be borne by our Northern brethren as resulting from our system of Government; and they cannot attack the institutions of slavery without attacking the institutions of the country, our safety, and welfare." In other words, white southerners regarded abolitionists as irresponsible fanatics intent on deluging Dixie with blood by fomenting slave revolts.[38]

The deterioration of relations between the North and South heightened these fears, and southern newspapers fed the apprehensions of their readers by giving credence to rumors of slave revolts. This sensational but vague account from the December 20, 1856, edition of the *Southern Shield* of Helena, Arkansas, typified the genre:

Great alarm has existed in many localities in the South in regard to contemplated servile insurrections. In some instances, developments have been made which leave no doubt that serious outbreaks may have occurred but for the timely and extremely fortunate discovery of the fiendish plans concocted by misguided and ignorant blacks.... Atrocious murders of whole families might have been committed ... at the first outbreak, but it would have ultimately resulted in certain death to the perpetrators—for it is idle for the slave population ... to think that an insurrection can result in anything but destruction to all who engage in it.

The antislavery mass-murderer John Brown seemingly provided irrefutable confirmation of these fears when he seized the Federal arsenal at Harpers Ferry, Virginia, in mid-October 1859 in an abortive effort to launch a slave revolt massive and bloody enough to terrorize the South into ending the "peculiar institution." The fact that so many white northerners hailed Brown as a martyr after his conviction and hanging in Virginia convinced their southern cousins that they would never be safe as long as they remained in the Union. By that time, southerners equated the Republican Party with the abolitionist movement. When Abraham Lincoln, a Republican dedicated to the containment and gradual elimination of slavery, won the White House in November 1860, that was enough to turn secession from a threat into a reality.[39]

At the opening of the Civil War, Lincoln insisted that he was waging a crusade to save the Union as it existed in 1860—with slavery as a sacrosanct state right. Racial hysteria left Confederates impervious to his words, but such a message reassured the North's War Democrats, who rallied around the Stars and Stripes to strike down secession and rebellion, but not the peculiar institution. As the struggle stretched into the summer of 1862, however, Lincoln decided that emancipation was necessary to undermine the Confederate war effort. When Lincoln coupled his Emancipation Proclamation of January 1, 1863, with an open appeal to African Americans to join the Union Army, it seemed as if the Confederacy's worst nightmare was about to become reality. If, as southern whites believed, blacks were ungovernable savages, then Lincoln's decision to arm them meant total war—war against white southern men, women, and children. This new northern policy inflamed Confederates in the same way that the British use of Indians to raid the colonial frontier infuriated earlier generations of Americans during the Revolution and the War of 1812.[40] Twelve days after Lincoln promulgated the Emancipation Proclamation, Jefferson Davis told the Confederate Congress that the measure was really designed to encourage southern slaves to rise in "a general assassination of their masters." The Confederate president added that Lincoln's initiative deserved to be regarded as "the most execrable measure recorded in the history of guilty man."[41]

The southern press echoed Davis's outraged sentiments. The *Washington Telegraph* in Washington, Arkansas, roundly denounced "the crime of Lincoln in seducing our slaves into the ranks of his army" as "amongst those stupendous wrongs against humanity, shocking to the moral sense of the world, like Herod's massacre of the innocents, or the eve of St. Bartholomew." Situated in the more cosmopolitan Little Rock, the *Arkansas Gazette* proclaimed with grim firmness,

"Our course is plain. A savage war has been forced upon us. We will have to meet, and deal with it as we find it." The competing *True Democrat* agreed that Lincoln had initiated "a war for extermination, not only of men, but of women and children." The *Gazette* went so far as to urge the Confederate government to adopt a draconian policy: "Arming negroes, as soldiers or otherwise, or doing any thing to incite them to insurrection is a worse crime than the murder of any one individual: Therefore, all officers and soldiers willingly serving in armies guilty of such practices, . . . should be punished as murderers."[42]

The fact that these crude racial stereotypes lacked factual substance did not prevent Confederate soldiers and civilians from clinging to them. Delusion was part of the price that the white South paid for slavery, as it allowed the master class and its dependents to live with an immoral labor system and to applaud indefensible conduct on the battlefield.

Belief in a savage and inhumane enemy makes soldiers feel that they are absolved from treating such opponents according to the rules of war. Such sentiments had inspired Anglo-American troops to massacre Indian combatants and noncombatants on numerous occasions since the 1600s. These same fears made it almost inevitable that Confederate troops would commit atrocities when they encountered elements of the U.S. Colored Troops. On one level, the killing of wounded and captured black soldiers represented acts of vengeance against men Confederates viewed as renegades who had dared to raise their hands against their masters. In a more important sense, Rebel troops viewed these merciless acts as a distasteful but essential form of race control. It was better to kill those African Americans who had defected to the enemy in order to deter a wholesale slave revolt.[43]

The *Washington Telegraph* exhibited this sort of thinking when it justified the massacre of members of the 1st Kansas Colored Infantry (later known as the 79th U.S. Colored Infantry) following the Battle of Poison Spring, Arkansas, on April 18, 1864: "It follows irresistibly that we *cannot* treat negroes taken in arms as prisoners of war, without a destruction of the social system for which we contend. In this we must be firm, uncompromising, and unfaltering. We *must* claim the full control of all negroes who may fall into our hands, to punish with death, or any other penalty, or remand to their owners. If the enemy retaliate, we *must* do likewise; and if the *black flag* follows, the blood be upon their heads."[44] An Arkansas cavalryman who witnessed the Poison Spring Massacre expressed the lesson to be learned from it in a letter to his wife: "Our men is determine[d] not to take negro prisoners, and if all of the negroes could have seen what occurred

The Fort Pillow Massacre, wood engraving in *Harper's Pictorial History of the Civil War* (New York, 1866). The Fort Pillow Massacre was remembered in print and image during and immediately after the war, but over time slavery as the cause of the war and blacks' contributions to Union victory were eclipsed in rituals of reconciliation and remembrance of the war as a noble brothers' fight. This image survived in a chromolithograph made by Louis Kurz and Alexander Allison and published in 1892. The firm of Kurz and Allison produced a series of dramatic battle scenes that included black soldiers in heroic or tragic poses, which reminded Americans of blacks' role in the fight and of a wartime outrage that should not be forgotten. (Library of Congress)

that day, they would stay at home." Black soldiers repaid the Rebels in the same coin when they could, and the escalating violence prompted a white Union officer stationed in Arkansas to write his wife, "It would not surprise me in the least if this war would ultimately be one of extermination. Its tendencies are in that direction now."[45]

Lincoln had remarked many times about the vicious racial prejudice that in-
fected his America, and he had to know that unleashing the Union's sable arm
would provoke a cycle of atrocity and reprisal. After all, the Rebel populace had
greeted invading Federal forces during the war's first year with fierce guerrilla
resistance that frequently transgressed the rules of war. Even a man far less intelligent than Lincoln had to expect that adding black soldiers to such a highly
charged environment would add more fuel to his enemies' fury. The sixteenth
president had been born in Kentucky, which made him a son of the South. He
was fully aware of the region's fears and prejudices. Experience had probably also
taught him that there was no gentle way to uproot slavery from American soil,
and permitting black men to participate in the trauma-ridden process was probably the best way to assure them a place in the postwar order. While Confederates bear the primary responsibility for their own war crimes, the Union president could have done more to deter them. Lincoln responded to Rebel threats to
re-enslave captured black soldiers and the inevitable reports of racial massacres
by promising to respond in kind, but he shied away from any open retaliation.
He seemed to think that African Americans in uniform would find their surest
protection in the destruction of the Confederacy. At the same time, he wanted to
avoid worsening the lot of white Federals in enemy hands.[46]

The Lincoln administration did cite the Confederate refusal to treat black soldiers according to the rules of war as an excuse for shutting down an already
brittle prisoner-of-war exchange system. In one respect, this represented shrewd
strategy. Refusing to exchange captured Rebel troops prevented an outnumbered
Dixie from replenishing the shrinking ranks of its army—while the more numerous North could find plenty of fresh recruits and draftees to replace its losses.
Lincoln ignored the murder of captured black troops on the battlefield to avoid
creating a cycle of retaliation that would engulf white Union prisoners as well.
He could have easily continued the exchange system for the same reason, but
doing otherwise paid immediate military dividends. At the same time, however,
this policy change carried a tragic price. It deliberately exposed tens of thousands
of men in blue and gray to needless suffering and death. Because neither side
was willing to devote sufficient resources to make their prison camps healthy
installations, the surest way to keep POWs alive was to speedily parole them to
friendly lines, where they would remain out of combat until finally exchanged.
In addition to closing this safety valve, the Lincoln administration reacted to the
Fort Pillow Massacre of April 12, 1864, the most publicized war crime involv-

"The Emancipation of the Slave," bas-relief of the Cuyahoga County Soldiers' and
Sailors' Monument, Cleveland Public Square, 1894. This monument unites the
various strands of Lincoln leadership, pointing to his image as emancipator, commander in chief, and president, all supported by the service of soldiers and sailors
in winning the war. The strong hands holding the musket attest to military force
needed to bring victory, and suggests that the black soldier pledging loyalty to the
cause is an incipient citizen. Such monuments in public squares across the North
attested to the central place accorded Lincoln's leadership and the resolve to stand
together against any threat to the nation.

ing the U.S. Colored Troops, by drastically slashing rations in northern prison
camps. Lincoln had full knowledge of this covert revenge policy, and he never
lifted a finger to end it. These were cold-blooded measures, and we must remember them as elements of the kind of war Abraham Lincoln waged.[47]

Nothing said here should unseat Lincoln as the greatest war president in
American history. He identified his mission as preserving the Union—humanity's
last chance for a free future—and he let nothing stop him from accomplishing
it. He defined the office of commander in chief—something the Constitution
failed to do—by exercising unparalleled powers. He bore the burden of leading

his people through an agonizing ordeal, and he attempted to bind up the nation's wounds even before the guns fell silent.[48]

Nevertheless, it is well to remember that war means suffering, something from which this nation remains largely insulated, even after a decade of military engagement in Afghanistan and Iraq. Those who lead their nations to war are impelled to make hard decisions that cause immeasurable pain. Any evaluation of their performance must factor that consideration into the equation. After all, armed conflict needs to be judged in a different light than sporting events, which are often treated as its analogical equivalent. A proper sensitivity to humanity demands that we disprove the lament of the poet Walt Whitman, who worked as a nurse in a Union Army hospital: "Future years will never know the seething hell . . . of the Secession War; and it is best they should not—the real war will never get in the books."[49] That sort of self-censorship only makes it easier to start new wars—and that should never be easy. Thus, when we call Abraham Lincoln an outstanding war leader, we must never forget that means he excelled at a hellish business. He had to run his hands through rivers of blood before history could place the conqueror's laurel on his brow.

3

Seeing Lincoln's Blind Memorandum

Matthew Pinsker

A few days after his reelection on Tuesday, November 8, 1864, President Abraham Lincoln made a startling revelation to his inner circle. According to the diary of aide John Hay, the president "took out a paper from his desk" at the Friday morning cabinet meeting, and said, 'Gentleman do you remember last summer I asked you all to sign your names to the back of a paper of which I did not show you the inside? This is it." Lincoln then directed Hay to open the mysterious note, which had been "pasted up in so singular a style that it required some cutting to get it open." The text of the document, dated from the Executive Mansion on Tuesday, August 23, 1864, read in its entirety: "This morning, as for some days past, it seems exceedingly probable that this Administration will not be re-elected. Then it will be my duty to so co-operate with the President elect, as to save the Union between the election and the inauguration; as he will have secured his election on such ground that he can not possibly save it afterwards."[1] The sixty-word statement had been signed "A. Lincoln" and was endorsed on the reverse side by the seven cabinet officers at that time. Postmaster General Montgomery Blair, one of August signers, had since been fired. Lincoln now explained to the others that his original purpose had been to outline a "course of action," which he had "solemnly resolved on" during a period "when as yet we had no adversary, and seemed to have no friends." Lincoln described how he had been expecting the Democrats to nominate General George McClellan, and planned in the event of Little Mac's victory to confront his former subordinate "and talk matters over with him." Lincoln suggested that he had been prepared to concede that McClellan was "stronger" and had "more influence with the American people than I," but since he retained the "executive power of the Government" until March 4, the two men would need to work together "to try to save the country." Lincoln's proposal to McClellan would have been straightforward: "You raise as many troops as you possibly can for this final trial, and I will devote all of my energies to assisting and finishing the war."

Hay refrained from commenting on this unprecedented offer, but the twenty-seven-year-old made sure to include within his diary a withering response from

Secretary of State William Henry Seward, by far the most astute politician in the cabinet. "And the General would answer you 'Yes, Yes,'" replied Seward, "and the next day when you saw him again & pressed these views upon him he would say 'Yes—yes' & so on forever and would have done nothing at all." To this prediction, Lincoln merely observed, "At least I should have done my duty and have stood clear before my own conscience."[2]

If anybody else spoke up, Hay did not record it. Nor did any of the other diarists present capture the episode for posterity. There also seems to have been no direct account from August when the president had first asked the seven men to endorse something they were not allowed to read, and no other type of contemporary testimony from November when Lincoln finally explained the document's purpose to the remaining six men. The adviser who finally broke the code of silence was the former secretary of the navy Gideon Welles in a reminiscence he contributed to the *Atlantic Monthly* in 1878. Welles labeled the document a "desponding note," and paraphrased it briefly to illustrate how badly things had looked by August 1864. "At no time had Mr. Lincoln been more depressed," he concluded.[3]

Welles's account irritated John Hay, who was then living in Cleveland and preparing to write an official biography of Lincoln with his former Executive Mansion colleague John G. Nicolay. Hay was jealously protective of the original document, which he still had in his possession. "Do you understand Mr. Welles' reference to a 'Memorandum,' written by Lincoln in 1864 in anticipation of defeat, in [the] Atlantic?," he complained to Nicolay. Hay reported that he had "the whole occurrence in my notebook" but regretted that he had once distributed copies of the August 23 note to a few of the cabinet officers. "I cussed silently," he recalled, when the outgoing attorney general Edward Bates and then Welles had requested keepsakes of the document following the November 11, 1864, meeting, implying that he had long suspected it would eventually make for wonderful postwar memoir material. "I have been dreading their reappearance," he added about the copies, with the tartness of an author in the process of being scooped.[4]

When Nicolay and Hay finally published their ten-volume masterpiece on Lincoln in 1890, they did succeed in turning the August 23 memo into one of their more dramatic set-pieces. Though agreeing with Welles that the period had been one where "the general gloom and depression enveloped the President himself," they did far more to flesh out the details of that political despair in late 1864—not only by publishing for the first time the text of the actual document, but also by providing excerpts from starkly pessimistic reports that Lincoln had received in the days just preceding his unlikely pledge of cooperation.[5]

When annotating the short text of the note, which they labeled "Memorandum Concerning His Probable Failure of Re-election," Roy P. Basler and the editorial team from *The Collected Works of Abraham Lincoln* (1953) included nearly all the supplementary material used by Nicolay and Hay in their biography, creating a footnote that was more than ten times longer than the document itself.[6] The result of this unusual editorial action only increased the biographer's tendency to see this moment in psychological terms. Lincoln scholars James G. Randall and Richard N. Current, for instance, titled their chapter on this episode "Dark Summer" and described the note in dramatic terms as Lincoln's "pessimistic letter" and "remarkable memorandum."[7] The episode continues to serve as a convenient way for biographers to illustrate what they perceive as Lincoln's depressed state of mind in August 1864. Over the years, there has been some disagreement over what (and whom) he feared most, but there has been little debate that the president was in a dour mood. The historian Mark E. Neely Jr. made one notable innovation to an otherwise static story line by effectively renaming the document as the "blind memorandum" in a widely read state-of-the-field essay published in 1979.[8] Although Neely's reference was slightly miscast—in modern bureaucratic custom a "blind memorandum" is unsigned, not unseen—the terminology has since become the norm. In his Pulitzer Prize–winning study *Battle Cry of Freedom* (1989), James M. McPherson writes, for example, that Lincoln "fully anticipated defeat in November," and thus, "on August 23 he wrote his famous 'blind memorandum' and asked cabinet members to endorse it sight unseen."[9]

But this chapter suggests that Lincoln's cabinet members are not the only figures who have struggled to see this blind memorandum clearly. Lincoln's biographers have too easily used this complicated document in ways that overstate his electoral anxieties and underestimate his tightly controlled reelection strategy. If Lincoln was truly anticipating defeat, then why did he not take more dramatic (and politically obvious) action in August, such as stepping aside as the Union nominee or flip-flopping on his most unpopular policy positions? This would have been the moment, for example, when a lesser political figure would have abandoned emancipation or at least opened negotiations with the Confederacy in order to encourage public prospects for peace. By rejecting these more politically attractive options in the face of an "exceedingly probable" election defeat, Lincoln appears in retrospect not depressed as much as uniquely determined to stay the course. But what was his political course by this stage in the war? And

"That's What's the Matter, or Who's to Blame—A Tragedy," by Henry Louis Stephens, *Phunny Phellow* 4, no. 4 (February 1863). Critics in the Republican Party blamed Lincoln for the war's military failures, mismanagement, a discouraged public, and the unrealized promise of emancipation. Republicans in Congress sought to insert their own interests by creating oversight committees, such as the Joint Committee on the Conduct of the War, which became forums for criticizing the administration. Such critics encouraged challenges to Lincoln's reelection in 1864, as Republicans of all stripes worried that he could not win and that with him on the ticket Republicans would lose in congressional and state elections. (Harris Civil War and Slavery Collection, Providence Public Library, Special Collections, Providence, RI)

what exactly did he intend by having cabinet members sign the note without reading it? The blind memorandum provides a useful opportunity to showcase both the full range of Lincoln's political skills and also the depth of his principles. The president often acted alone, nearly always dominated his cabinet, and routinely outmaneuvered his rivals because he was so obsessive about details and so meticulous about understanding the perspectives of others. The document also reveals a profoundly principled politician who refused to cancel or ignore an election whose outcome he feared might destroy the nation. The blind memorandum provides much more than a dramatic snapshot of a bad summer; it opens a unique and revealing window into the full panorama of Lincoln's political leadership.

Understanding Lincoln's achievement as a political leader begins with an acknowledgment that he was not only a self-made man, but also a self-made politician. "You must do like Seward does," he was once advised by "Long" John Wentworth, the legendary Chicago mayor and political boss. "Get a feller to run you."[10] But unlike his former rival William Henry Seward, Lincoln never had a Thurlow Weed. The truth is that he never needed one. From his first campaign at the age of twenty-three until his last race thirty-two years later, Lincoln won seven out of ten contests, mainly on his own initiative and guided by his own political instincts. And the two "defeats" he suffered in U.S. Senate contests (1854–55, 1858–59) were not really defeats at all, but rather party setbacks handed to the Republicans in an era when legislators selected senators almost always along strict partisan lines. That is how Lincoln was able to claim in his 1859 autobiographical sketch that his first electoral defeat in 1832, at the age of twenty-three, was "the only time I ever have been beaten by the people." Along the way, there were always some Lincoln political intimates—usually self-proclaimed—but none who seemed to stay with him from one stage of his career to the next. His law partner William H. Herndon was the classic example. Herndon was an original Lincoln man who worked side by side with the future president for seventeen years before the senior partner left for Washington and then hardly interacted with him again.[11]

The singular style of Lincoln's wire-pulling, coupled with his "shut-mouthed" nature, has complicated the process of writing his political narrative. Especially on questions as nuanced as those involving the blind memorandum, the Lincoln historian is often left with few reliable sources. The challenge is to reconstruct what the British historian Maurice Cowling has called the "sociology of power."[12] Historians must take into account the competing agendas of Lincoln's various cronies and offer reasonable speculation about the motivations of his actions. The basis for such analysis often comes as much from what is not written or done as it does from actual texts or actions.

Consider the "blind" August 23, 1864, endorsement by the cabinet officers. What might have motivated such powerful men to sign a document "sight unseen"? Perhaps Lincoln had really succeeded in forging a "team of rivals," to use the phrase popularized by Doris Kearns Goodwin. Or perhaps the peculiar nature of the endorsement—a kind of nineteenth-century date stamp—made knowledge of its contents seem irrelevant to the signers. But a different explanation might highlight the disjointed and disgruntled nature of that cabinet. Salmon P. Chase, the longtime secretary of the treasury, had not been one of the "blind" signers, because Lincoln had fired him earlier that summer once the president had secured his renomination. Maybe that decisive action had opened a few eyes. Lincoln's hard edge was certainly apparent in the firing of Montgomery Blair, who did sign the August document but who was let go just a month later, presumably as part of an implicit bargain to remove the third-party candidate John C. Fremont from the presidential race. Nothing better demonstrates the awkward chemistry of this cabinet group than the realization—almost never expressed in the scholarship—that regardless of their motivations for signing, Lincoln must have demanded "blind" endorsements from his cabinet because he did not trust his closest subordinates to keep such an explosive statement secret. This significant distrust would also help explain their bewildered reaction to the president's dramatic revelation about the memorandum's contents in November 1864.

Analyzing the power relationships within the administration and the Union coalition is especially challenging during the 1864 campaign. There were a bewildering variety of party organizations supporting the president, from the regular state and national Republican committees to a veritable maze of ad hoc Union Leagues.[13] Elected officials, cabinet members, newspaper editors, independent operators, army officials, and government agents all claimed roles in the campaign and were prone to bitter divisions over everything from ideology to patronage to regionalism to Jacksonian-era party affiliations—even to family feuds. Lincoln gave hardly any public speeches or published interviews during the contest, but met almost daily with friends and rivals to discuss political questions. Meanwhile, the campaigns that truly mattered were still being fought on the battlefields—often with frustrating results for a weary northern public. Thus Lincoln's victory over George McClellan inspired more relief than celebration. The president himself soberly concluded that the election had been a "necessity," and that he was gratified by the "right conclusion" to an otherwise divisive contest.[14]

Over the years, there have been several hotly disputed points of interpretation regarding the campaign. The sudden collapse of the presidential boom for Treasury Secretary Chase generated much attention at the turn of the twentieth

"Presidential Cobblers and Wire-Pullers Measuring and Estimating Lincoln's Shoes," *New York Illustrated News*, March 5, 1864. This oft-referenced cartoon casts Lincoln's rivals and critics as lilliputians looking for a replacement nominee for the presidency. Eight of the persons depicted were newspaper publishers. The Radical Republican and popular antislavery orator Charles Sumner is also in the band. Surprisingly, the cartoon also includes William Henry Seward, who was a strong Lincoln supporter by 1864, which fact contributed to the Radicals' disgust with Lincoln and Salmon P. Chase's ambition to unseat him. (Library Company of Philadelphia)

century. In the 1890s, the Pennsylvania journalist Alexander McClure and the former presidential aide Nicolay launched a debate that continued for decades over whether Lincoln engineered the replacement of his vice president, Hannibal Hamlin, with the Tennessee War Democrat Andrew Johnson. Historians in the twentieth century also investigated the deal that allegedly got Fremont out of the race in exchange for the removal of Postmaster Blair from the cabinet.

But interpreting the blind memorandum has not proved nearly as controversial as these well-known debates. According to nearly all the standard accounts,

the president's darkest moment came in late August when stalemate on the battlefield had spooked many northern Republicans into contemplating the possibility of dumping him from the Union ticket. The failure of Grant's armies to
capture Richmond during the summer, growing discontent on Capitol Hill over
Reconstruction policies, and the recent announcement of another half-million-
man call-up seemed to have deflated almost everyone. Even Lincoln himself, according to the usual plotline, feared the worst and was preparing for the likeli-
hood of his own defeat until General William T. Sherman's capture of Atlanta
in early September transformed public opinion and saved his reelection.[15] Yet
under closer scrutiny, it appears that while many around the president were
clearly alarmed over his prospects, he remained confident, or at least unshaken.
All of his previous political experience had taught him that despite the sound
and fury of his increasingly forlorn campaign team, his position as the regular
party nominee was practically unassailable. For Lincoln, the only serious question concerned whether he could win at the polls without his generals gaining
any more victories in the field. Despite expectations to the contrary, it was a
question the president seemed prepared to answer with a tactic that showed his
more anxious contemporaries a glimpse of the worst. In other words, Lincoln
spent most of August attempting to scare his more lukewarm allies straight. The
blind memorandum was in effect a culmination of this strategy.

One of the best illustrations of this tactic in action occurred on Friday, August 19, 1864. It was a typically full day for the president, with an agenda that
included a perfunctory cabinet meeting as well as discussions with the abolitionist Frederick Douglass and the former Wisconsin governor Alexander Randall.
The meetings with Douglass and Randall were anything but perfunctory, however, since the topic of discussion in both cases was a politically charged letter that Lincoln had drafted regarding peace negotiations with the Confederacy.
The question had become more and more pressing during the period of military
stalemate, and Lincoln had reluctantly authorized a series of secret, back-chan-
nel missions to sound out Jefferson Davis. In public, however, Lincoln remained
resolute about negotiations. In a general statement issued on July 18, 1864, Lincoln had announced that "any proposition" which included the "integrity of the
whole Union" and the "abandonment of slavery" would be considered by his
administration. Naturally, such a hard line seemed to foreclose the possibility
of talks. It also suggested to some northern critics that emancipation had been
transformed from a temporary and somewhat limited policy of military necessity into a sweeping national political objective. In his August 19 meetings, the

president openly discussed a letter he was drafting in response to the particular concerns of Charles T. Robinson, a newspaper editor and leading pro-war Democrat from Wisconsin, who had challenged Lincoln to explain how he was supposed to convince his skeptical readers that saving the Union and "freeing the slaves" were now inseparable goals.[16]

Randall had delivered the confidential note from Robinson earlier in the week, and he and some associates planned to visit with Lincoln at the president's summer cottage at the Soldiers' Home on Friday evening to hear his draft response.[17] "To me it seems plain," Lincoln began, "that saying re-union and abandonment of slavery would be considered if offered is not saying that nothing else would be considered, if offered." But if Lincoln's opening gambit was designed to appeal to conservative sensibilities, the rest of the response was a passionate, often indignant, defense of his emancipation policy. "I am sure you would not desire me to say, or to leave an inference," Lincoln wrote in the original draft, "that I am ready, whenever convenient, to join in re-enslaving those who shall have served us in consideration of our promise." Lincoln might have hoped that such a balancing act would satisfy both conservatives and radicals, but he more likely had another plan in mind. He read the draft first to Douglass, and then to Randall's party, revised it at least once, but never sent it.[18]

Other scholars have commented on Lincoln's habit of drafting but not sending materials, usually in the context of angry outbursts aimed at wayward generals, but in this case the strategy seemed to have had a more calculated effect.[19] Lincoln wanted to bring his political allies around by showing them the war from his perspective and by offering a sign of how bad things would become if he went down in defeat. Nothing suggests this scheme more clearly than the meeting with Frederick Douglass at the White House on Friday morning. The orator had opposed efforts to renominate Lincoln and was actively considering supporting John Fremont. "When there was any shadow of a hope that a man of a more decided anti-slavery conviction and policy could be elected," Douglass wrote, "I was not for Mr. Lincoln."[20] By this point, Douglass was far from alone in his discontent. The day before, on August 18, a group of leading Radical Republicans had met in New York City at the home of former mayor George Opdyke to organize a movement that might be able to recruit a substitute for Lincoln as the Union candidate. "Mr. Lincoln is already beaten," Horace Greeley argued. "He cannot be elected. And we must have another ticket to save us from utter overthrow."[21] Aware for some time that such movements had been afoot, Lincoln had asked Colonel John Eaton, who supervised the escaped slaves or "contrabands" living behind Union lines in the Mississippi Valley, to arrange the meeting with Douglass.[22]

Once he heard the draft of Lincoln's answer to the conservative critics, Douglass's reaction was thoroughly predictable. The black abolitionist argued strenuously against Lincoln's proposed reply to Robinson. "It would be taken as a complete surrender of your anti-slavery policy," Douglass said, "and do you serious damage."[23] Lincoln listened but then wondered aloud if it was still possible to encourage more southern slaves to escape, since the war might end without the complete abolition of slavery. Douglass understood this to be a veiled threat.[24] The abolitionist returned home and reluctantly drafted a plan for a new "Underground Railroad," but the aspiring politician combined his reply with a request for a personal favor. He asked the president to discharge his son Charles from the army because of illness. Lincoln immediately ordered the discharge.[25] The president was not as imposing in his conversation that evening with Randall and the others, but he did become passionate at one point, denying that he could abandon emancipation even if he should do so for political reasons. "I should be damned in time & in eternity for so doing," he claimed adamantly.[26]

In retrospect, Lincoln's objective on August 19, 1864, seems clear. He was buying time, hoping that either better news from the front or sheer desperation would eventually restore a unity of purpose to his shaky political coalition. This latter, worst-case scenario often gets lost in the interpretive shuffle, drowned out by the agonized rhetoric of Lincoln's political lieutenants. As word of the Opdyke meeting leaked out, for example, Republican politicians like Henry Raymond, the *New York Times* editor and general campaign chairman, and even political war horses like Thurlow Weed, began sounding despondent tones in letters that have been widely quoted since the publication of Nicolay and Hay's official biography and their subsequent inclusion in the annotations for the *Collected Works*. Weed wrote Seward on August 22, 1864, reminding him that for days he had been calling Lincoln's election "an impossibility" because the "people are wild for peace." On the same day, Raymond sent the president a long, depressing note outlining the party's poor prospects in various states and warning that the "tide is setting strongly against us."[27]

But was Lincoln equally disturbed and unsettled? He certainly appeared in full command of his moods on August 19, 1864. Scholars occasionally cite a thirdhand account passed along to General Benjamin Butler, a man who aspired to become the new Union candidate, which suggested that the president might have been persuaded to step aside. "You think I don't know I am going to be beaten, *but I do* and unless some great change takes place *badly* beaten," Lincoln reportedly told one visitor. Yet if true, that statement was made much earlier in the month.[28] There are more signs that by mid-August the frustrations of the summer were serving mainly to increase Lincoln's determination. Illinois Lieutenant Governor William Bross visited the White House during this period on his way to recover the body of his brother who had been killed at Petersburg. He tried to offer the president some political advice, but was cut short. "I will tell you what the people want," said Lincoln sharply. "They want and must have, *success*. But whether that come or not, I shall stay *right here*, and do my duty."[29] To another old Illinois friend, Lincoln appeared at times almost indifferent to the political crisis around him. Leonard Swett, an instrumental Lincoln organizer during the realignment of the 1850s, recalled that he "poured [himself] out" to the president about the forlorn campaign, only to watch in disbelief as Lincoln gazed absentmindedly out of a window, imitating a nearby bird: "Tweet, tweet, tweet; isn't he singing sweetly?" Swett reported that he felt "as if my legs had been cut from under me," and rose angrily to leave until Lincoln called him back, saying by way of apology, "It is impossible for a man in my position not to have thought of all those things."[30]

Lincoln's candor with his old Illinois friends hints at a likely truth. Always a meticulous political manager, he was now verging on obsession in his attention to the details of his final campaign—and with no sign of surrender. Nothing better demonstrates the level of Lincoln's preoccupation and determination than the blind memorandum, which involved an elaborate example of worst-case planning. By noting that it seemed "exceedingly probable that this Administration will not be re-elected," Lincoln offered an opening line that sounded the alarm in much the same way as all the other reports from that week. But if Lincoln was truly shaken, as his correspondents appeared to be, then the next line should have read, "Therefore I have decided for the sake of my party and country to step aside as the Union nominee." Instead, Lincoln announced that it would be his "duty to so co-operate with the President elect as to save the Union between the election and the inauguration." To fully appreciate the surprising nature of that statement, one must acknowledge that the pressure on Lincoln *at that moment* was to resign or step aside as his party's choice for president. By refusing to do so, as he signaled in this document, Lincoln was defying many powerful political forces within his own party.

In crafting the memorandum, Lincoln was also defying some of his closest allies, the ones who did not want him to step aside but who did press him to

Platforms Illustrated (Philadelphia, [1864]), lithograph attributed to Prang and Company. Republicans cast themselves as the true American party, and contrasted their steadfast commitment to defeat secession while disparaging the Democrats as a party in trouble because of its supposed dominance by Copperheads and party bosses, a reluctant candidate in George B. McClellan, and a reliance on the immigrant vote. This lithograph shows Liberty crowning Lincoln, who is held aloft by the pillars of Union strength. (Library of Congress)

change his policies. Lincoln avoided the alternative policy options recommended by his advisers. Some pushed him to abandon emancipation. Others urged him to open negotiations with Richmond. Lincoln appeared to consider these ideas, but ultimately embraced none of them. During the same week that he revised the Robinson letter and prepared the blind memorandum, Lincoln was also pulling together a document authorizing Raymond to open talks with Jefferson Davis. Yet none of these materials saw the light of day in 1864. Lincoln might have been serious in contemplating these alternatives, but more likely he was engaging in a political Kabuki dance to help others see their futility. The blind memorandum offers especially powerful evidence that Lincoln had become almost disdainful of compromise and flip-flops by this point in the war. Consider how he was offering in the memorandum to "co-operate" with the Democratic president-elect, but could not resist adding in this otherwise magnanimous note that his opponent would "have secured his election on such ground that he can not possibly save it afterwards." In his 1979 essay, Mark Neely suggested that this bitter edge marked "the real operative content of the memo"—namely, that Lincoln was "a loyal Republican and shared his party's fears of a disloyal opposition."[31] From this perspective, Lincoln certainly appears far more radical than pragmatic—a revealing insight for a man and a leader often celebrated for his conciliatory nature.

Thus, when the ever-pragmatic Henry Raymond and other leading members of the Union executive committee finally arrived at the Executive Mansion on August 25 to confront the president about his resistance to a peace mission and secure final authorization for a new mission to Richmond, he dismissed them rather easily. Along with what John Nicolay labeled the "stronger half of the Cabinet," which included, in the aide's view, Seward, Edwin Stanton, and the new treasury secretary, William Pitt Fessenden, the president provided a "respectful answer" to the committee's various political concerns but essentially killed plans for negotiations, somehow leaving them both "encouraged and cheered." Writing to Hay, who was back home in Illinois during this period, Nicolay observed, "If the President can infect R. and his committee with some of his own patience and pluck, we are saved."[32]

They were soon saved, and Lincoln's "patience and pluck" was a critical element of their salvation. The Opdyke movement began collapsing even before the news of Sherman's victory reached the North. Governor John Andrew of Massachusetts pulled out of the cabal in late August. Even if Lincoln would have stepped aside, which he almost certainly would not have, then who could have united the disparate factions? Chase and Fremont certainly could not. Generals like Grant or Butler might have in theory, but Lincoln kept careful tabs on both. Grant repeatedly made clear that he would not serve as a candidate. Besides, why nominate generals whose troops were mired in stalemate? After all, that was the problem presumably eroding most of Lincoln's popularity in the first place. Nor is it conceivable that the coalition's members would have splintered or simply accepted defeat. There was just too much at stake. Weed's explanation for why he refused to join the movement exposes the fatal flaw in the plans to dump Lincoln. "Knowing that I was not satisfied with the President, they came to me

Miscegenation; or, The Millennium of Abolitionism (New York, 1864), lithograph by Bromley and Co. One of four political caricatures issued by the Bromley firm for the Democratic Party, this lithograph repeated the Democratic charge that emancipation meant racial mixing and a social order turned upside down. Democrats used racial stereotypes as regular campaign fare, especially after emancipation became Republican policy, to paint Lincoln and the Republicans as dreamers and fanatics. The frustrations with military reverses and the cost of the war, worries about violations of civil liberties, and racial fears proved a potent combination, leading to Democratic successes in local, state, and congressional elections in 1862 and 1863, which worried Republicans that they might lose the White House and more in 1864. (Library of Congress)

for cooperation," he wrote to Seward on September 20, 1864. "But my objection to Mr. Lincoln is that he has done too much for those who now seek to drive him out of the field."[33] James Gordon Bennett, the astute editor of the *New York Herald*, had outlined the outcome on the very day Lincoln was penning the blind memorandum. The various Republican factions would be "skedaddling for the Lincoln train and selling out at the best terms they can," the paper predicted, "because the president has the whiphand of them." Bennett concluded, "The spectacle will be ridiculous; but it is inevitable."[34]

Inevitability is an argument easy to make afterward. But if historians focus on the sociology of power rather than the mood swings of the chattering classes, it does appear easier to see what Lincoln saw. He was going to remain the Union nominee with or without victories in Atlanta or Richmond. If there was any political turning point, it was the Republican decision, orchestrated by Lincoln supporters, to hold an early convention in June and the subsequent Democratic move to delay their gathering from mid-July to late August. Imagine if the meetings had been reversed. A Democratic convention held during the initial enthusiasm surrounding Grant's Wilderness Campaign might have resulted in diminished influence for the Peace Democrats and a more acceptable general election platform. A Republican or Union convention at the end of August would have provided Lincoln's critics with a rallying point and real opportunity.

Nonetheless, just because Lincoln was likely to remain the nominee even without battlefield victories does not mean that he would have won in November. That is the final reason why the blind memorandum appears so remarkable. Lincoln wrote the document as a last-ditch attempt to secure a policy victory even if he endured a personal defeat. After a month spent opening the eyes of friends, he was now planning for the prospect of scaring his political enemies straight, too. Few interpretations of the blind memorandum bother to dissect Lincoln's extraordinary and extra-constitutional offer for a coalition government during the period of lame-duck transition, but he clearly believed the proposal would have had an impact on McClellan and Democratic Party leaders. Recall Lincoln's imagined conversation with President-Elect McClellan as recounted in Hay's extraordinary diary entry: "Now let us together, you with your influence and I with all the executive power of the Government, try to save the country. You raise as many troops as you possibly can for this final trial, and I will devote all my energies to assisting and finishing the war."[35] In the event of his possible electoral defeat, what Lincoln wanted was a statement from McClellan urging regular troops to stay in the field and encouraging northern civilians to respond positively to the latest call up of more men. What Lincoln feared most was that absent such a public endorsement, the Union Army would collapse from the weight of postelection desertions and increasing unrest on the home front. This explains the earnest and careful nature of the August 23 document, most especially those mysterious blind endorsements. Lincoln understood full well that McClellan and his advisers would be inherently skeptical of his motives. From

Grand National Union Banner for 1864: Liberty, Union, Victory (New York, 1864),
lithograph with watercolor by Currier and Ives. Running under the National
Union Party label, the Lincoln-Johnson ticket played up themes of military might,
harvest, commerce, and progress rather than remarking on emancipation or
responding to Democrats' politics of race. The message was that the reelection of
Lincoln would restore the Union and ensure its future happiness, as related in this
banner with its farmer plowing a field and cornucopia spilling abundance. (Library
of Congress)

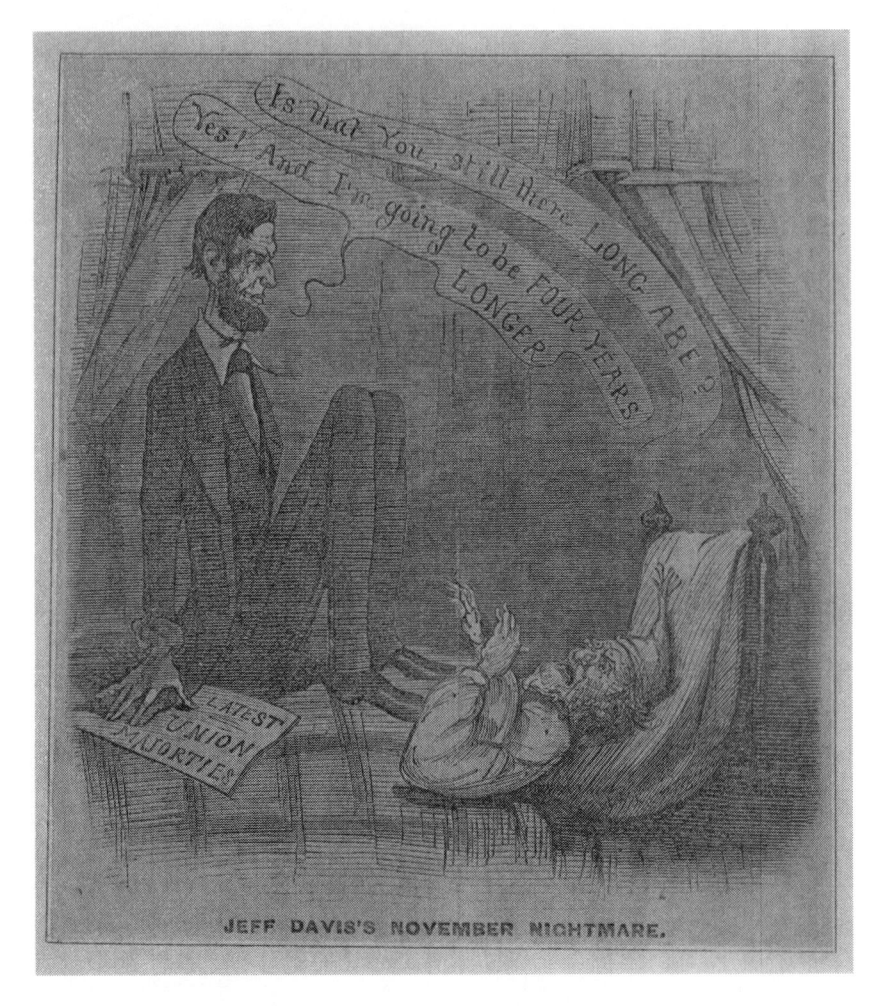

"Jeff Davis's November Nightmare," *Frank Leslie's Illustrated Newspaper*, December 3, 1864. This cartoon spoke a great truth, for the Confederacy had counted on Lincoln and the Republicans' defeat in the 1864 elections as the best chance for a negotiated peace and the prospect of realizing southern independence. Lincoln ran hard on the need to win the war at all costs and never to concede any legitimacy to secession. Strengthened by electoral victory in 1864, thanks in part to the soldiers' vote, Lincoln determined to finish what in the Gettysburg Address he had called "the great task remaining before us." (Library of Congress)

their perspective, President Lincoln—who had suspended habeas corpus in defiance of the Chief Justice, and imprisoned thousands of citizens without judicial process, and who had, as they saw it, emancipated slaves by military decree in the unconstitutional fashion of John Brown—was utterly capable of ignoring election results and holding power indefinitely. Thus, the blind memorandum, with its impromptu "date stamp" secured by the unknowing cabinet officers, revealed that Lincoln had been reconciled to a possible electoral defeat for months while simultaneously offering an ominous reminder to the incoming team that unless they found some way to cooperate with him, chaos awaited them in March 1865.

Following his reelection, President Lincoln quietly informed a serenade of supporters outside the Executive Mansion, "We can not have free government without elections."[36] This was not mere rhetoric. By deciding to forge ahead with his campaign during the panicky days of late August, Lincoln demonstrated that a long and successful career in politics had girded him to resist self-doubt and ignore public criticism. He did not step aside under pressure as the Union nominee. Nor did he flip-flop on key policies. Most important, he did not cancel the election. Any of those choices might have fatally undermined his legacy. Instead, the evidence suggests that Lincoln only pretended to consider depressing alternatives in order to draw allies—and sometimes enemies—back into his fold. Yet none of this speculation about tactics or analysis regarding the "sociology of power" should obscure the fact that Lincoln's decision to commit himself wholly to the verdict of the people at the moment when his own prospects seemed dimmest marks one of the most inspiring examples of popular sovereignty in American history. That is surely how Lincoln saw the blind memorandum—and how he hoped history would view it. "At least," he had confided to his stunned cabinet officers after the election, "I should have done my duty and have stood clear before my own conscience." The self-conscious pride of that statement has long merited more careful examination. There should no longer be much doubt that August 23, 1864, was a decisive day in Lincoln's presidency, full of insight about both his unparalleled partisan skills and unyielding faith in the people.

4 Abraham Lincoln as Moral Leader

The Second Inaugural as America's Sermon to the World

Harry S. Stout

This chapter addresses the subject of Abraham Lincoln as a moral leader in the context of both the Civil War and nineteenth-century standards of morality. Such a topic, if handled thoroughly, would require an entire book addressing such themes as just-war planning for Civil War campaigns, just-war conduct, treatment of civilians and of prisoners of war, slavery and racism, and so on. For purposes of this chapter, I will select only one aspect of Lincoln's moral vision and leadership, namely, his Second Inaugural Address, which I take to be the single most eloquent moral commentary on the war.

It is one of the curiosities of Lincoln's historiography that his Second Inaugural Address was not widely analyzed until recently. Far more attention was paid to Lincoln's Gettysburg Address. There were few conferences devoted to the inaugural address or sustained scholarly publications on it. Indeed, not one book-length study of the Second Inaugural was published before the twenty-first century. Then, in one year, two books appeared that explored the many dimensions of the 701-word Second Inaugural: James Tackach's *Lincoln's Moral Vision: The Second Inaugural Address*, and Ronald White's *Lincoln's Greatest Speech: The Second Inaugural*.[1] Missing from these books, however, is the sermonic—even Puritan—dimension of the address.

While we technically label Lincoln's Second Inaugural an "address," or, in Ronald White's title, a "speech," contemporaries and scholars agree that it was really a sermon in all but name. Immediately following the oration Lincoln asked Frederick Douglass what he thought, to which Douglass replied, "Mr. Lincoln, that was a sacred effort." Later, Douglass explained the reason for the power of the speech: "The address sounded more like a sermon than a state paper."[2] Later historians such as Mark Noll, Ronald White, Allen Guelzo, and Richard Carwardine agree. Like Martin Luther King's "I Have a Dream" speech, the cadences, phraseology, biblical allusions, and deep moral stirrings bespeak more the pulpit than the podium.[3]

Considered as a sermon, there is only one early American competitor for the label America's greatest sermon, Jonathan Edwards's *Sinners in the Hands of an Angry God*. I have taught the *Sinners* sermon for over thirty years now, but always in isolation as an aspect of Edwards's rhetoric. But the more I pondered Lincoln's Second Inaugural, the more it dawned on me that despite obvious differences, there are important similarities between the two, which yield unique insights into Lincoln's address.

In linking Edwards and Lincoln, I recognize that in many ways they could not be more different. Edwards is the theologian of damnation that liberal thinkers from Mark Twain forward have loved to hate. And Lincoln, the martyred prophet, is the theologian of reconciliation that Americans have loved to love. Yet in one respect the two sermons share a remarkable thematic overlap. Both are concerned, even obsessed, with guilty Americans in the hands of an angry and vengeful God. It is true we do not often think of Lincoln's charitable Second Inaugural in the same vein as Edwards's *Sinners*. But I believe that an angry God holds the key to unlocking the innermost meaning of both addresses. More particularly, it forms the indispensable prelude and context to charity toward all and malice toward none. Without an angry God there would be no occasion for charity and forgiveness.

At key points in the Second Inaugural, Lincoln introduces themes of transgression and divine punishment on a wayward people. Most directly it appears in the prophetic, biblically based judgment, "Woe unto the world because of offences! For it must needs be that offences come; but woe to that man by whom the offence cometh!" Lincoln's handwritten text punctuated the quote with exclamation points. They signal trouble—biblical trouble—with an angry God voicing the charge.[4]

The trigger for God's anger is slavery. Indeed, by 1865 it had become the driving moral cause of the war. In words allowing for no ambiguity, Lincoln devotes the third paragraph to the proposition that "slaves constituted a peculiar and powerful interest [to the South]. All knew that this interest was, somehow, the cause of the war." This conclusion is startling for its singularity. It is not paired with the preservation of the Union as dual and reinforcing causes, but as *the* cause. As such it represents a radical departure from themes articulated in Lincoln's First Inaugural, when the preservation of the Union was the driving moral

"The 'Sunken Road' at Antietam," stereograph by Alexander Gardner, 1862. The cruel reality of the war's harvest of death, as shown in this depiction of Confederate dead in a ditch, caused many people to seek religious explanations for the slaughter and suffering. The human cost made Lincoln all the more reflective on what God and history were demanding of the nation he once termed "the last best hope" of humankind. Lincoln approached his second inauguration determined to give the great sacrifices meaning. (Library of Congress).

cause of the war. The tone of Lincoln's First Inaugural was less prophetic than legal, and the sole issue he addressed was the preservation of the Union. Lincoln left it to the South whether they would remain in the Union with slavery intact and at peace, or secede from the Union and bring war.[5]

By 1863 this had changed. First there was the Emancipation Proclamation, taking effect on January 1, 1863, and then the Gettysburg Address in November. In his prize-winning analysis of Lincoln's Gettysburg Address, Garry Wills identified how Lincoln subtly changed the legal compromise at the heart of the Constitution, bringing it to its own indictment. In Wills's words, Lincoln "performed one of the most daring acts of open-air sleight-of-hand ever witnessed by the unsuspecting. Everyone in the vast throng of thousands was having his or her intellectual pocket picked. The crowd departed with a new thing in its ideological luggage, that new constitution Lincoln had substituted for the one they brought there with them. They walked off, from those curving graves on the hillside, under a changed sky, into a different America. Lincoln had revolution-ized the Revolution, giving people a new past to live with that would change their future indefinitely."[6]

Surely Wills is correct in his assessment, but the redefinition did not stop with the Gettysburg Address. The Second Inaugural completes the sleight of hand. Just as Lincoln at Gettysburg subtly rewrote the Constitution from a document of compromise with the Devil to a "new birth of freedom," so Lincoln trans-

"Lincoln Delivering His Second Inaugural Address as President of the United States, Washington, D.C.," photograph by Alexander Gardner, 1865. Lincoln is standing in the center of the photograph. The large crowd gathered at the inau-guration expected a message of triumph to celebrate Union success in arms and the prospect of restoring the Union on a victor's terms. Lincoln did not know yet when the war would end. In his Second Inaugural he insisted that the war God had willed might continue until all the debts and sins of the nation had been settled, and he urged the nation to "finish the work we are in." (Library of Congress)

formed the cause of the war in his Second Inaugural from secession to slavery, which begat secession.

With slavery as the new or ultimate cause, Lincoln turns his attention to the southern slaveholders who owned the slaves for which this war was waged. In words that surely surprised his listeners, he again turns to Scripture with sentiments the opposite of judgment: "It may seem strange that any men should dare to ask a just God's assistance in wringing their bread from the sweat of other men's faces; but let us judge not that we be not judged." When I first read this quote—really read it—I responded as I imagine many hearers at the time did. What? Are you serious? This from the man who famously remarked, "I am naturally anti-slavery. If slavery is not wrong, nothing is wrong."[7] And now he's telling us not to judge southern slaveholders for their "peculiar" sin? Surely this is understatement on a grand scale. Why pick this time and occasion to pull punches he leveled at the institution for his entire life? And why shouldn't the ones fighting a war to contain and then end slavery judge the result with approbation?

Here we come to the central moral paradox animating the speech. Lincoln opens his address with an accusation and a refusal to judge because, as he makes the case, all white Americans collectively share in the guilt of slavery. In yet another sleight of hand, Lincoln substitutes the collective "we" for the "ye" of the King James Bible. Never has one changed word made a greater difference. Judgment is not an individual charge or a regional charge, but a collective sin. Lincoln was saying that if we concentrate on judging the evil of the slaveholding South, we miss the message that God wants to leave the broken nation with: that *all* of us are responsible for this war because all of us were or are complicit in the evil of slavery. All of us are *not* guilty of secession, but we share a collective guilt for slavery. Without the active participation—and profit—of the North, the institution would have foundered. Southern planters had been saying this for years, but now the same sentiment springs from the highest seat of power in the North. The language of judgment is inclusive. There are no innocents. And that is why God is an equal opportunity accuser, judging both North and South, with war as the penalty. As common sinners, Lincoln could hold forth the promise of eventual reconciliation as common friends.

While conceding the nobility and moral gravitas of these words and sentiments, it is important to note their moral limitations as well. Lincoln's position, while deeply ethical, is arguably not the only moral position to take on the issue of judgment. While Lincoln was right about the white North and the white South

Vol. IX.—No. 429.]   NEW YORK, SATURDAY, MARCH 18, 1865.

LINCOLN TAKING THE OATH AT HIS SECOND INAUGURATION, March 4, 1865.—PHOTOGRAPHED BY GARDNER, WASHINGTON.—[SE

"President Lincoln Taking the Oath at His Second Inauguration," *Harper's Weekly*, March 18, 1865. This image of Lincoln, swearing on the Bible to uphold the Constitution, represented the twin foundations many Republicans invoked to carry on the war and to define Reconstruction. (Library of Congress)

sharing complicity in the sin of slavery, there were others who were virtually guilt free and who therefore could justifiably stand outside the judgment prohibition. I am referring, of course, to African Americans. Whether enslaved or free, they felt the betrayal of slavery and racism, with the equal assurance that they had done absolutely nothing to deserve such a fate. *Their* morality would not be so forgiving. Roughly 195,000 African Americans fought and roughly 37,000 died for one overwhelming end: the abolition of slavery and protections for the black race from a racist culture bent on violent suppression. We like to label Lincoln the "Great Emancipator," but in truth emancipation was an African American project as much as a Republican project, and too many biographies of Lincoln err in so elevating Lincoln's role in abolition as to marginalize the thousands who stood in the storm for three centuries. Their voices and their consciences must also be heard in conversation with Lincoln.

Frederick Douglass admired Lincoln in many ways and even counted him a friend, but he was not in a forgiving mood. While praising Lincoln's Second Inaugural as sermonic, Douglass also had profound issues with regard to its implication for African Americans. *He* was not guilty, and therefore stood outside the circle of Lincoln's white audience. In the view of Douglass and other abolitionists, too much forgiveness would lead to too much acceptance. And too much acceptance would lead to re-enslavement by different means. As long as the Union was the nation's ultimate priority—not abolition and racial equality—racism would endure. Douglass minced no words: "The law and the sword cannot abolish the malignant slaveholding sentiment which has kept the slave system alive in this country during two centuries. Pride of race, prejudice against color, will raise their hateful clamor for oppression of the negro as heretofore. The slave having ceased to be the abject slave of a single master, his enemies will endeavor to make him the slave of society at large."[8] Douglass was right. For a brief time, the Radical Republicans' and abolitionists' alternative vision of judgment and remaking the South bore promise. But tragically, it would not last. As David Blight has shown in his powerful book *Race and Reunion*, any real reconciliation of a (racist) North and South "could not have been achieved without the resubjugation of many of those people whom the war had freed from centuries of bondage. This is the tragedy lingering on the margins and infesting the heart of American history from Appomattox to World War I."[9]

And it was precisely that trade-off of race and reunion that led Douglass to oppose any unpunished reconciliation with the former Confederacy. Lincoln's

The Rail Splitter at Work Repairing the Union (New York, 1865), lithograph by Currier and Ives. By the time of Lincoln's Second Inaugural, popular print was already celebrating Lincoln for his moral strength and resolve in completing the mighty task of saving the nation. (Library of Congress)

promise of leniency and speedy reconciliation did not bode well for African Americans. It seemed to Douglass that after the government had asked "the Negro to espouse its cause and turn against his master," it now planned to "hand the Negro back to the political power of his former master, without a single element of strength to shield himself."[10]

Having established what Lincoln meant when he refused to judge the South, and now that we understand the racial limitations of his inclusive refusal to judge, we can move on to a second question: Why was the rhetoric of an angry God so *powerful* in the American consciousness? Why did it strike resonant chords in a nineteenth-century American culture? Because if nothing else, an angry God is a *personal* acting God, and that meant a God in relationship to a collective people.

Deistic "first causes" or clock-maker deities do not get angry; they are distant and aloof, working through the inviolable laws of nature. In 1865 this was not Lincoln's God. From this speech and other earlier ruminations, it is clear that any vestige of an impersonal, fatalistic deism on Lincoln's part had long left his mind, to be replaced by the more Puritan God of the Hebrew Bible, who entered into covenants with chosen nations and judged them when they broke the terms. An angry God is an engaged—and enraged—God. And, paradoxically, that is both terribly scary and gloriously affirming of a national divine chosenness.

Of course, Lincoln's God was still a far cry from Edwards's evangelical God. Edwards's angry God was concerned with individual souls with an eternity of hell's torments standing in the balance. Like Lincoln, Edwards was a master wordsmith. Here is one example of how Edwards in *Sinners* portrayed an angry God holding guilty sinners to judgment:

> The wrath of God burns against them, their damnation don't slumber, the pit is prepared, the fire is made ready, the furnace is now hot, ready to receive them, the flames do now rage and glow. The glittering sword is whet, and held over them, and the pit hath opened her mouth under them . . . the devil is waiting for them, hell is gaping for them, the flames gather and flash about them, and would fain lay hold on them, and swallow them up; the fire pent up in their own hearts is struggling to break out . . . there are no means within reach that can be any security to them. In short, they have no refuge, nothing to take hold of, all that preserves them every moment is the mere arbitrary will, and uncovenanted forbearance of an incensed God.[11]

Unlike Edwards's Northampton, Massachusetts, congregation who had heard hellfire before, his Enfield, Connecticut, audience was encountering him for the first time when he delivered his now famous sermon. And unlike Lincoln, Edwards was so terrifying that he could not even conclude his sermon as the shrieks and agonies of his terrified listeners forced him to stop.

Lincoln's angry God was not concerned with individual souls, but rather the nation-state as a collective people, and the consequences were less individual damnation for eternity (which Lincoln didn't believe in) than hell on earth: the hell of slavery's bondage for over two hundred years on the part of the slaves, and the hell of a retributive civil war with death and unprecedented destruction as the calamitous price to be paid.[12] For Lincoln no less than Edwards, the wrath of God burned white hot. For Lincoln no less than Edwards, the divine sword glittered, before striking a million predominantly young male sinners into the pit. And there was no place to hide. No wonder, in the immediate aftermath of the address, Lincoln wrote to Thurlow Weed, "I believe it [the Second Inaugural] is not immediately popular. Men are not flattered by being shown that there has been a difference in purpose between the Almighty and them. To deny it, however, in this case, is to deny that there is a God governing the world. It is a truth which I thought needed to be told; and as whatever of humiliation there is in it, falls most directly on myself, I thought others might afford for me to tell it."[13]

In Puritan categories, Lincoln's address was less a Sunday salvation sermon like Edwards's *Sinners*, than an occasional fast-day sermon directed to the national state of affairs. Nevertheless, precisely because God was personally angry with (white) America, therein lay the evidence of affirmation that He had chosen the United States for some great destiny. This rhetorical pattern, elaborated on by the scholars of Puritanism Perry Miller and Sacvan Bercovitch, became labeled the "American jeremiad."[14] It went like this: since God chastises only those whom He loves, the judgments of the Lord confirmed sacred nationhood even as they proclaimed doom and gloom. The Puritans' jeremiad, and Lincoln's jeremiad, attested to the larger truth that God had chosen the United States for some great, messianic destiny. And Lincoln was not about to squander that destiny as the "world's last best hope."

Lincoln began the Second Inaugural by telling his listeners that he could not tell them when the war would end, as so many earlier broken assurances had done. He could not tell how many more would be sacrificed to satisfy the mortal debt incurred by the sin of slavery. But in 1865 he knew that at some point the war would be ended. And he knew further that the Union would be preserved to engage its sacred destiny.

In nineteenth-century evangelical culture in the United States, a personal God was a providential God—a God actively involved in orchestrating the affairs of humankind for His mysterious ends. Briefly stated, the doctrine of Providence made room for direct divine intervention in the affairs of humankind. Calvinists believed not only that God was absolutely sovereign but also that God intended to use that sovereignty to influence the course of events in nature and among His human creation. In this view God could and did affect everything from famines and droughts to victories and defeats, as a form of divine pedagogy to teach wayward Christians the errors of their ways. This doctrine shaped what we might call today psyches. Providence prepared Americans to accept any level of suffering because, ultimately, it was not human agency that governed the outcome of events, but divine strategy.[15]

Providence may have been mysterious. But all knew it was real. They knew as well that God was just and therefore unable to allow national sins to go unpunished. And finally they knew that once God was angry there was no place to hide. Humankind was helpless before an angry God.

As sobering as providential rhetoric no doubt was to nineteenth-century Christians, it becomes more problematic for twenty-first century students. With notable exceptions, we as a culture no longer hold such a providential view of war. This is where I believe it is possible to see the downside of the jeremiad. Consider this famous phrase from the Second Inaugural, which again comes right from Scripture: "Yet, if God wills that it continue, until all the wealth piled by the bondsman's two hundred and fifty years of unrequited toil shall be sunk, and until every drop of blood drawn with the lash, shall be paid by another drawn with the sword, as was said three thousand years ago, so still it must be said 'the judgments of the Lord, are true and righteous altogether.'"[16] We might label this perspective a providential fatalism. This rhetoric enabled Lincoln and clergy on both sides to endure unimaginable suffering without blaming themselves for organizing the destruction. After all, it was not they who were orchestrating the events of this cruel war, but God, so whatever was, was. The human agents cannot ultimately be held to account for something God is directing. Who is to question the judgments of God in extending this war?[17]

In a solitary moment of meditation in 1862, Lincoln reflected on the mysterious meaning of God's providence:

> In the present civil war it is quite possible that God's purpose is something different from the purpose of either party—and yet the human instrumentalities, working just as they do, are of the best adaptation to effect His purpose. I am almost ready to say this is probably true—that God wills this contest, and wills that it shall not end yet. By his mere quiet power, on the minds of the now contestants, He could have either *saved* or *destroyed* the Union without a human contest. Yet the contest began. And having begun, He could give the final victory to either side any day. Yet the contest proceeds.[18]

Even as Lincoln's sense of Providence grew stronger, the destruction around him escalated out of control, provoking a sort of feeding frenzy of violence. There was Cold Harbor, where soldiers perished at a rate of sixty per minute, and Spotsylvania, where, for twenty-three hours, two entire corps of soldiers faced off at fifty yards, throwing themselves at one another in a savage death dance during which communications were impossible, lines unformed, and men fought desperately for their lives. There were the anguished cries of farmers, women, children, and the elderly watching their farms razed and houses burned. All with no enemy army in sight! Nobody questioned it. Why? It seemed like the greater the suffering the more removed the moralists became from the cruelty. Like Lincoln, clergy on both sides retreated into a providential mantra that allowed them to escape personal responsibility for the escalation. Ministers on both sides of the conflict, in overwhelming numbers, were, in effect, held captive to the state and willingly allowed themselves to be engines of mobilization for the war effort— by failing to ask hard questions about the war's unjust conduct, and uncritically "praying to the same God" for legitimation and victory.

True, there were exceptions. In the North, a clerical writer for the *New York Evangelist* on April 23, 1863, mused on the morality of the war in ways that anticipated the Second Inaugural, and in some ways even went beyond it in targeting racism as well as slavery as the common property of North and South:

> The war has been permitted as a punishment to both the North and the South. Both have been guilty, though in different ways and in different degrees. We trust that God will overrule it for good to both, but it will not be because either deserve it. . . . There is one sin the North is committing toward the blacks, that needs to be repented of. It is not slavery, but it is the denial of the rights of men to the poor unfortunate negroes who are among us . . . we are called as a people to acknowledge the full manhood of the negro race.

Unlike Edwards's *Sinners*, which saw listeners running for the exit, the immediate response to Lincoln's Second Inaugural was muted. Secular commentators concentrated on Vice President Andrew Johnson's inebriation, and clerical voices groused that they were not included on the platform. Nevertheless, I would suggest that Americans *did* get it. It sounded for all the world like a fast sermon, and they heard so many of those that the prose was not immediately electrifying. But surely it took root.

It is not at all clear to me that we Americans today would be as swayed by the logic of the jeremiad in the face of massive casualties (if translated into figures relative to today's larger population of more than three hundred million persons counted in the United States, "massive" would total over six million war deaths!).[19] And here allow me to make a brief digression. I recently wrote a moral history of the Civil War titled *Upon the Altar of the Nation*. For twelve years I explored this vexed question from all angles. Throughout, a question that drove me was how could things get so out of hand? I thought to myself, they were Americans; I'm an American; they were just like me. So how did it happen that hundreds of thousands could kill hundreds of thousands? The usual explanations didn't satisfy me. Emancipation didn't explain it; Union didn't explain it; secession didn't explain it.

Only after reading countless sermons, religious newspapers, fast-day proclamations, children's literature, and music scores did it finally dawn on me. They *weren't* just like us! They were a people and a nation profoundly different. And nowhere was this difference more pronounced than in their resignation to a theological prism they may not have even been able to self-consciously articulate as theological, but nevertheless was theological and profoundly biblical. At the center of this prism was a surrender of ultimate responsibility for their actions. Only people who believed that events controlled them, rather than vice versa, could resign themselves to a passive—if enraged—acceptance of what transpired in the war. As Lincoln confided in a letter to Albert G. Hodges, in April 1864, "I claim not to have controlled events, but confess plainly that events have controlled me."[20]

Today we certainly know how to kill, and in that sense share common ground with those in the nineteenth century, and all of humanity for that matter. But there still exists today a sense of personal agency. Deep down we know that atrocities are the tragic consequences of our own actions, deliberate or inadvertent. It is precisely for this reason that we may have prosecutions against individual actors for war crimes and crimes against humanity. Nineteenth-century Americans were blind to personal agency as ultimate cause. The divine and supernatural light of divine agency blinded even one as empathetic and loving as Abraham Lincoln. All eyes saw the burning glory of the coming of the Lord. All knew with certainty that He was trampling out the vintage where the grapes of wrath are stored; and that He had loosed the fateful lightning of His terrible swift sword. And no one knew it better than Abraham Lincoln.

If the Second Inaugural was a staple of nineteenth-century American religion and a fast jeremiad at heart, it was brilliantly condensed and eloquent, even poetical, as so many commentators have observed. And because the fast was so

FROM OUR SPECIAL WAR CORRESPONDENT.

"City Point, Va., *April* —, 8.30 A.M.
"All seems well with us."—A. Lincoln.

"From Our Special Correspondent," *Harper's Weekly*, April 15, 1865. By spring, many people who had earlier been his critics revered Lincoln. Though critics still abounded, Lincoln's death caused people to turn to admiring Lincoln's gifts, especially as a writer and a person with an unusual empathy for the sufferings of others. Such appreciation added to the significance of Lincoln's Second Inaugural, giving it for many the character of a last commandment from the nation's prophet. (Library of Congress)

familiar, it was not immediately canonized as American scripture. For that to happen would require Lincoln's assassination and subsequent memorialization. In other words, it would require the messianic nobility of the speaker to inscripturate the nobility of the speech.

Only after excoriating the nation for two hundred years of slavery can Lincoln move forward to a collective compassion in the manner of Christ's Sermon on the Mount. Without an angry God judging both North and South, there would be no occasion for charity and forgiveness, because one side was "right" and the other "wrong," and therefore the right side had a right to judge—and further punish—the wrong. But if all are guilty, a different response is called for: "With malice toward none; with charity for all; with firmness in the right, as God gives us to see the right, let us strive on to finish the work we are in; to bind up the nation's wounds; to care for him who shall have borne the battle, and for his widow, and his orphan—to do all which may achieve and cherish a just, and a lasting peace, among ourselves, and with all nations." There is no evidence that Lincoln prayed to or had a love for Jesus as personal savior, no matter how much later evangelicals claimed. His God was the God of the Old Testament and the Hebrew chosen people. But if he was not a Christ lover, he knew Christ's rhetoric well and adopted it as his own.

Lincoln closed his sermon with a plea for peace "with all nations." These last three words address his sense of the obligation of the United States to the world. They distinguish Lincoln from the other nineteenth-century unifier, Otto von Bismarck, Germany's "Iron Chancellor." As I understand Bismarck's campaign, it was engaged purely for the pragmatic creation of a powerful nation state whose preservation and perpetuation was its own highest end. This mentality persisted and would drag Germany into devastating wars of national aggrandizement. In contrast to this Machiavellian hyper-nationalism was Lincoln's engagement "with all nations." Lincoln believed passionately in the U.S. republic. It was his "political religion," and one that he hoped would be preached to the world. But it was not nationalism for the sake of nationalism. As Allen Guelzo demonstrates, Lincoln's was a prudential and moral nationalism.[21] Put simply, he would never have said "my country, right or wrong." The United States, Lincoln believed, deserved reverential awe only to the extent that it conformed to the higher ethical imperative contained in the principle that "all men are created equal." That is why he said repeatedly that if the nation could survive only "half slave and half free," including the territories and states-in-waiting, that it was a republic not worth preserving.

With that as his conclusion, we may conclude, with Ronald White, that the Second Inaugural was Lincoln's greatest speech. It provided future generations with the interpretive and mythic context that not only explained the United States to itself but also explained the United States to the world. In ways both literal and symbolic, the Second Inaugural captured the deepest strains of the

The Last Moments of Abraham Lincoln, President of the United States (Philadelphia, 1865), hand-colored lithograph by Max Rosenthal. The public's deification of Lincoln came quickly with his death, or "martyrdom" as many people came to describe it. That Lincoln was shot on Good Friday added to the feeling that God ordained his life and death. This image, with reverent cabinet members and generals contemplating Lincoln's death and angels beckoning him to heaven, all below the approving visage of the sainted George Washington, rolled into one the image of a sanctified Lincoln and nation and gave his last words, as in the Second Inaugural, greater resonance. (Indiana Historical Society, P0406)

nation's transformation. With the sin of slavery fairly exposed and the suffering made understandable, the way was cleared to embark on a new path—a path that, as many have recently pointed out, has led to the nation's forty-fourth president. I don't know if the Civil War has finally ended. In fact, I doubt it. But it marks a significant and irreversible step forward.

Appendix: Text of the Second Inaugural

Fellow-Countrymen:

At this second appearing to take the oath of the Presidential office there is less occasion for an extended address than there was at the first. Then a statement somewhat in detail of a course to be pursued seemed fitting and proper. Now, at the expiration of four years, during which public declarations have been constantly called forth on every point and phase of the great contest which still absorbs the attention and engrosses the energies of the nation, little that is new could be presented. The progress of our arms, upon which all else chiefly depends, is as well known to the public as to myself, and it is, I trust, reasonably satisfactory and encouraging to all. With high hope for the future, no prediction in regard to it is ventured.

On the occasion corresponding to this four years ago all thoughts were anxiously directed to an impending civil war. All dreaded it, all sought to avert it. While the inaugural address was being delivered from this place, devoted altogether to saving the Union without war, urgent agents were in the city seeking to destroy it without war—seeking to dissolve the Union and divide effects by negotiation. Both parties deprecated war, but one of them would make war rather than let the nation survive, and the other would accept war rather than let it perish, and the war came.

One-eighth of the whole population were colored slaves, not distributed generally over the Union, but localized in the southern part of it. These slaves constituted a peculiar and powerful interest. All knew that this interest was somehow the cause of the war. To strengthen, perpetuate, and extend this interest was the object for which the insurgents would rend the Union even by war, while the Government claimed no right to do more than to restrict the territorial enlargement of it. Neither party expected for the war the magnitude or the duration which it has already attained. Neither anticipated that the cause of the conflict might cease with or even before the conflict itself should cease. Each looked for an easier triumph, and a result less fundamental and astounding. Both read the same Bible and pray to the same God, and each invokes His aid against the other. It may seem strange that any men should dare to ask a just God's assistance in wringing their bread from the sweat of other men's faces, but let us judge not, that we be not judged. The prayers of both could not be answered. That of neither has been answered fully. The Almighty has His own purposes. "Woe unto the world because of offenses; for it must needs be that offenses come, but woe to that man by whom the offense cometh." If we shall suppose that American slavery is one of those offenses which, in the providence of God, must needs come, but which, having continued through His appointed time, He now wills to remove, and that He gives to both North and South this terrible war as the woe due to those by whom the offense came, shall we discern therein any departure from those divine attributes which the believers in a living God always ascribe to Him? Fondly do we hope, fervently do we pray, that this mighty scourge of war may speedily pass away. Yet, if God wills that it continue until all the wealth piled by the bondsman's two hundred and fifty years of unrequited toil shall be sunk, and until every drop of blood drawn with the lash shall be paid by another drawn with the sword, as was said three thousand years ago, so still it must be said "the judgments of the Lord are true and righteous altogether."

With malice toward none, with charity for all, with firmness in the right as God gives us to see the right, let us strive on to finish the work we are in, to bind up the nation's wounds, to care for him who shall have borne the battle and for his widow and his orphan, to do all which may achieve and cherish a just and lasting peace among ourselves and with all nations.

5   Lincoln and Leadership: An Afterword

Allen C. Guelzo

Shortly after his arrival in Washington in late February 1861, Abraham Lincoln was confronted by an anxious delegation from a national peace conference that was even at that late moment hoping to head off the national gallop toward civil war. They were not unfriendly; many of the conference's members were, like Lincoln, old-time Whigs from the Upper South and the border states. But they wanted some statement from Lincoln about the policy he would adopt toward the seven southern states that had declared their secession from the Union, a statement that they could add to the oil they were trying to spread on the nation's troubled waters. Bafflingly, Lincoln replied that he was still too unacquainted with the situation to make any statements about policy. He informed them "that he was accidentally elected president of the United States"—*accidentally*, in this case, meaning that his election was the result of the three-way splintering of opposition candidates who had thus ensured his election by default—"that he had never aspired to a position of that kind; that it had never entered into his head; but that from the fact of his having made a race for the Senate of the United States with Judge Douglas in the state of Illinois, his name became prominent, and he was accidentally selected and elected afterwards as president of the United States."[1] He was, in other words, simply unprepared to offer them anything—direction, hope, even hostility.

The delegation listened to this with a healthy degree of incredulity, and so do we. We do not elect presidents because they lack ideas, but because the majority of the citizenry agree with the ideas the candidates take so much trouble to articulate. But in some senses Lincoln was speaking more truly than his hearers credited. His election *had* been something of an electoral fluke. He carried only 39 percent of the popular vote in the election of 1860 (although that 39 percent was concentrated in northern states with rich electoral-college representations, which could probably have elected him even if the three rival candidates had banded together on one ticket). Even more, his nomination by the Republican national convention came from far, far behind the pack of front runners like William Henry Seward and Salmon Chase. He had twice, unsuccessfully, run for the

U.S. Senate, in 1855 and again in 1858. He had never been a governor (like Seward and Chase)—never even mayor of his hometown of Springfield. And as Gregory Urwin reminds us, he was entering the presidency with only the slightest experience in military affairs, and at a time when military acumen was liable to become his greatest need. Stood up against his opposite number, the new provisional president of the Confederate States, Jefferson Davis, Lincoln looked ineffective, fumbling, and indecisive. Davis, at least, was West Point–educated, a former U.S. senator, and had been an innovative and capable secretary of war under President Franklin Pierce.

And yet Lincoln's presidency became (along with Thomas Jefferson's and Franklin Roosevelt's) one of the "hinge" presidencies of American history. He reoriented the relationship of government and business through public financing of a transcontinental railroad, protective tariffs, a new national banking system, and "homestead" legislation that converted vast stretches of the public lands in the West to commercial development. In Lincoln's hands, government became a supportive ally of business rather than an uncooperative neutral party. He became the first president to embrace the use of "war powers" by a commander in chief, thereby beginning a debate over the meaning and extent of those powers that continues to this day. And he swiftly emerged as a jealous guardian of executive privilege. He rebuffed with equal firmness attempts by his cabinet, Radical Republicans in Congress, and his generals to seize decision making from his hands. Caleb Blood Smith, Lincoln's first secretary of the interior, complained that "Mr. Lincoln doesn't treat a Cabinet as other Presidents—that he decides the most important questions without consulting his cabinet."[2] Smith was not exaggerating. For the previous six decades, overmighty cabinet secretaries had acquired increasing amounts of discretion and initiative, while executive authority languished. Lincoln decisively subordinated his cabinet secretaries to his own dictate as president, and thus laid down the outlines of cabinet-style administration that we live with yet.

To have done all this, while at the same time directing a four-year-long civil war, emancipating 3.5 million slaves, and deflecting bitter, almost-treacherous opposition from his critics, is enough to persuade almost anyone that Lincoln's election might have been "accidental," but the man himself was not. And indeed, locked within the shambling, ungainly appearance was an array of character assets that hardly anyone at the time suspected Abraham Lincoln possessed:

Persistence: Lincoln once remarked that he was a slow walker, but never walked backwards. The one lesson that he had learned from his father (who otherwise had few lessons that Lincoln cared to remember) was that the best way to deal with a bad bargain was to hug it tighter. This should not be mistaken, however, for mere unthinking stubbornness. As Matthew Pinsker's chapter tellingly illustrates, Lincoln was no pragmatist. He could conciliate, maneuver, and compromise with the best, but at the end of the process, Lincoln would still be adamant about the principles and goals that guided him. "I desire to so conduct the affairs of this administration," said Lincoln, "that if, at the end, when I come to lay down the reins of power, I have lost every other friend on earth, I shall at least have one friend left, and that friend shall be down inside of me."[3]

Resilience: Lincoln's long history as a trial lawyer had prepared him to lose as well as win, and any lawyer who could not live with loss had best seek out another line of work. As president, Lincoln was hammered with blows that would have broken almost anyone else. Shattering military defeats and lengthening casualty lists twisted anguished laments from him. After the death of his old friend Edward Dickinson Baker, at Ball's Bluff in 1861, the news "smote upon him like a whirlwind from the desert."[4] After the great loss at Chancellorsville in May 1863, the journalist Noah Brooks heard him cry out, "What will the country say? Oh, what will the country say?"[5] After the Union Army failed to finish off the Confederate Army at Gettysburg, he said to Navy Secretary Gideon Welles that "there is bad faith somewhere. . . . What does it mean Mr. Welles—Great God, what does it mean?"[6] And yet Lincoln absorbed these punishments the way a champion boxer absorbs the pummeling of his opponents, never at a loss for control, rarely responding in malice. "I shall do nothing in malice," he wrote in 1862. "What I deal with is too vast for malicious dealing."[7]

Humility: One key to Lincoln's resilience was his sense of proportion between his own self and the responsibilities of his office. Lincoln was far from being a political innocent; to the contrary, William Henry Herndon (his law partner for fourteen years) understood all too well that "Mr. Lincoln was a secretive man, had great ambition, profound policies, deep prudences . . . was retired, contemplative, abstract, as well as *abstracted*. . . . His ambition was never satisfied; in him it was consuming fire."[8] And yet he was capable of separating the internal craving for personal admiration and affirmation (which seems to be the common psychological deficit of all politicians) from the need to see a greater good being served. When he was slighted by George McClellan in 1862, Lincoln's secretary, John Hay, was amazed that Lincoln didn't pull his general's chain: "I would hold McClellan's horse," Lincoln replied, "if only he would give us victories." Nor did Lincoln nurse grudges. An amazed John Hay wrote in his diary, "It seems utterly

impossible for the President to conceive of the possibility of any good resulting from a rigorous and exemplary course of punishing political dereliction. His
favorite expression is, 'I am in favor of short statutes of limitations in politics.'"[9]
Ultimately, as Harry Stout's chapter reminds us, it was that humility that pulled
him, and the nation, back from the abyss of self-righteousness and triumphalism
at the end of the Civil War.

Knowledge: It is a common misperception that leadership is a spark of passion that falls from heaven on some single, foreordained head. In Lincoln's case,
"passion" seemed to be what he lacked most. "It is thought by some men that
Mr. Lincoln was a very warm-hearted man, spontaneous and impulsive," recalled
Herndon. "This is not the exact truth." Actually, "Lincoln dwelt entirely in the
head and in the land of thought. . . . He held his conscience subject to his head,
he held his heart subject to his head and conscience."[10] And in truth, leadership
must be based on the head—it requires exhaustive knowledge, acquired from
whatever means available. Passion, no matter how pure, cannot suffice as com-
pensation for ignorance. And this was certainly true of Lincoln. The Canadian
lawyer and journalist George Borrett was taken aback in 1864, when a visit to
Lincoln drew from the president "some shrewd remarks about the legal systems
of the two countries," and "a forcibly drawn sketch of the constitution of the
United States" and its "material points of difference" with "the political aspect
and constitution" of Great Britain.[11] Leonard Swett, who practiced law with Lincoln on the old Eighth Circuit in Illinois and who acted as a personal emissary
for Lincoln during the war, remembered that "whenever I would get nervous and
think things were going wrong," Lincoln had a comprehensive resource of facts
and figures to allay his doubts: "He kept a kind of account book of how things
were progressing for three, or four months, and he would get out his estimates
and show how everything on the great scale of action . . . the resolutions of Leg-
islatures, the instructions of delegates, and things of that character, was going exactly as he expected. . . . It was by ignoring men, and ignoring all small causes, but
by closely calculating the tendencies of events and the great forces which were
producing logical results."[12] This command of events, politics, and law provided
Lincoln with both direction and confidence. When John Hay asked whether he
was irritated at "the editorials in the leading papers" on the Emancipation Proclamation, Lincoln merely replied that "he had studied the matter so long that he
knew more about it than they did."[13] Knowledge not only told him the course
to take, but also armored him against the criticism of those who wanted him to
abandon the war or emancipation.

Loving the drudgery: Logan Pearsall Smith, the American-born British essay-
ist, once said, "The test of a vocation is the love of the drudgery it involves." He
might have been thinking of Lincoln in that regard, because Lincoln not only
knew both law and politics, but also rejoiced in the nuts and bolts of them. "The
leading rule for the lawyer, as for the man of every other calling, is diligence,"
Lincoln wrote in a lecture to aspiring lawyers. There were no shortcuts around
the drudgery of the law, Lincoln warned. "If any one, upon his rare powers of
speaking, shall claim an exemption from the drudgery . . . his case is a failure
in advance." Lawyering, he said in 1860, "is very simple, though laborious, and
tedious. . . . Work, work, work, is the main thing."[14] As a lawyer, riding the circuit,
he was often away from home as much as twenty-eight weeks in the year, and
it bothered him not a bit. David Davis, who sat as the presiding judge for the
Eighth Judicial Circuit, believed that "Mr Lincoln was happy—as happy as he
could be, when on this Circuit—and happy no other place."[15]

Persuasion: One final characteristic of Lincoln's leadership also grows out of
his experience as a trial lawyer, and that is his persuasiveness. As much as Lincoln acknowledged his "defective" education, he had more than made up for it by
his own program of self-administered learning, whether the subject was geology
or political economy, and by a marvelously retentive memory that permitted him
remarkable powers of recall. These he disciplined in the unforgiving school of
juries of farmers, mechanics, and merchants all across the Eighth Circuit and in
the state appeals courts. Jury pleading—and more than a thousand of the 5,173
cases for which Lincoln is the attorney of record went to jury trials—forced him
into the funnel of logical argumentation, clarity of expression, and transparent
earnestness.[16] "His legal arguments," wrote Isaac Newton Arnold, one of Lincoln's
warmest congressional allies, "were always clear, vigorous, and logical, seeking
to convince rather by the application of principle than by the citation of cases":
"He excelled in the statement of his case. However complicated, he would dis-
entangle it, and present the real issue in so simple and clear a way that all could
understand. Indeed, his [opening] statement often rendered argument unnecessary, and frequently the court would stop him and say: 'If that is the case, Brother
Lincoln, we will hear the other side.'"[17] As president, he turned from persuading juries to persuading public opinion, and he emerges from the mass of his
state papers as one of the most effective persuaders ever to occupy the presidential office. If for no other reason, wrote the Massachusetts abolitionist George
Boutwell, "Lincoln's fame will be carried along the ages" by "the proclamation
of emancipation, his oration at Gettysburg, and his second inaugural address."

These place him alongside "the noblest productions of antiquity, with the works of Pericles, of Demosthenes, of Cicero, and rivals the finest passages of Grattan, Burke or Webster."[18]

Taken together, these qualities do not necessarily "make" a Lincoln, since these are only the most salient markers of Lincoln's leadership, and since the operative balance between these markers is a formula locked in the recesses of Lincoln's own personality. But they do illuminate what is required for political leadership in a democracy. Unlike *monarchical* leadership, which is about honor, style, and the acquisition of power, or *bureaucratic* leadership, which is about efficiency, competence, and procedure, or *progressive* leadership, which is about empathy, image, and the embodiment of a communal will, a genuinely *democratic* leadership requires humor, humility, perspective, and resilience. And rarely has the combination been more fruitful, or more demanded by the moment, than in Abraham Lincoln. By 1863 John Hay thought that Lincoln had become a "backwoods Jupiter" who "sits here and wields . . . the bolts of war and the machinery of government with a hand equally steady & equally firm. . . . He is managing this war . . . foreign relations, and planning a reconstruction of the Union, all at once. I never knew with what tyrannous authority he rules the Cabinet, til now. The most important things he decides and there is no cavil." And yet, Hay added, "there is no man in the country, so wise, so gentle and so firm. I believe the hand of God placed him where he is."[19]

Hay's quasi-idolatrous sentiment has to be qualified by at least three deficiencies in Lincoln's presidential leadership. First, Lincoln was, to use a modern term, a workaholic. He suffered from what we might now diagnose as a mild form of depression, and his cure (that of many others in similar circumstances) was to turn his mind constantly to work. "Let me urge you, as I have ever done . . . in the depth and even the agony of despondency, [to] avoid being idle; I would immediately engage in some business, or go to making preparations for it."[20] As president, he believed that he was responsible even for answering the incoming mail (an illusion that his staff quietly dispelled). His oldest son, Robert Lincoln, recalled in 1918 that his father's "methods of office working were simply those of a very busy man who worked at all hours."[21]

Second, Lincoln's confidence in his mastery of the issues occasionally led him to the borderlands of unconscious arrogance. Leonard Swett told Herndon that "from the commencement of his life to its close, I have sometimes doubted whether he ever asked anybody's advice about anything . . . and when his opinion was once formed he never had any doubt but what it was right."[22] And John Hay, reflecting on Lincoln toward the end of Hay's own long and distinguished diplomatic career, admitted that Lincoln's "intellectual arrogance and unconscious assumption of superiority" was an irritant "that men like Chase and [Charles] Sumner never could forgive."[23] Nor was Lincoln always as much the master as he imagined he was. Gregory Urwin's chapter is a unique reminder that a great man cannot always be great in everything, and Lincoln's inexperience in military affairs may have been the weakest link in his chain. Not only did Lincoln meddle in the minutiae of command to an alarming degree, but he often did so based on strategic lessons that were long obsolete. Lincoln nagged commanders unmercifully about the need to come to grips with enemy armies in pursuit of a single, overwhelming, Napoleonic-style victory, and when his generals failed to do so, he darkly attributed their failure to political unreliability. But the day of the winner-take-all battle had faded decades before; victories were won not by smashing through enemy lines of battle, but by cutting lines of supply and support, and capturing the industrial centers that kept the armies in the field. It took Ulysses Grant and the Overland Campaign of May–June 1864 to convince Lincoln that the endless slugfest of battlefield armies was pointless, and that the real targets needed to be Atlanta, Richmond, and Mobile. When those places fell, the Confederate armies dropped in their tracks.

Yet, Herndon insisted, what these strengths and weaknesses created in Lincoln "was a perfect and an imperfect man, a strong man and a weak one; but take him all in all, he was one of the best, wisest, greatest, and noblest of men in all the ages." Ultimately, there is no single formula that explains Lincoln, or that allows us to identify another like him, and indeed most of the claims of politicians and presidents to have inherited Lincoln's mantle are not unlike the Frank Bellew cartoon (accompanying Matthew Pinsker's chapter), showing a crowd of lilliputian politicos trying to measure Lincoln's boots. But the example of how leadership grew from the meeting of a most unexpected man and our most dreaded hour is a reminder that no crisis is insoluble, and no field of counselors so unpromising but that one of them may indeed possess the single wisdom that the situation demands. Which is why, even as we toil through our own darkening political crises, we still look to the "bronzed, lank man" in the "suit of ancient black" that marks him as

> The quaint great figure that men love,
> The prairie-lawyer, master of us all.[24]

Notes

1. Lincoln and Leadership: An Introduction / Randall M. Miller

1. David Donald, *Lincoln Reconsidered* (New York: Vintage, 1956), 3–18.

2. On the Lincoln image and the various uses of Lincoln over time, see especially Merrill D. Peterson, *Lincoln in American Memory* (New York: Oxford University Press, 1994); Barry Schwartz, *Abraham Lincoln and the Forge of National Memory* (Chicago: University of Chicago Press, 2000); Barry Schwartz, *Abraham Lincoln in the Post-Heroic Era: History and Memory in Late Twentieth-Century America* (Chicago: University of Chicago Press, 2008); and David W. Blight, "The Theft of Lincoln in Scholarship, Politics, and Public Memory," in Eric Foner, ed., *Our Lincoln: New Perspectives on Lincoln and His World* (New York: Norton, 2008), 269–82. Also revealing about the enduring appeal, mystery, and uses of Lincoln is Harold Holzer, ed., *The Lincoln Anthology: Great Writers on His Life and Legacy from 1860 to Now* (New York: Library of America, 2009). For an eloquent assessment of Lincoln's relevance today, see James M. McPherson, "Lincoln's Legacy for Our Time," in Frank J. Williams and William D. Pederson, eds., *Lincoln Lessons: Reflections on America's Greatest Leader* (Carbondale: Southern Illinois University Press, 2009), 75–90. For a wide sampling of historians' recent takes on Lincoln's variable and enduring significance, see Brian Lamb and Susan Swain, eds., *Abraham Lincoln: Great American Historians on Our Sixteenth President* (New York: Public Affairs, 2008).

3. Donald, *Lincoln Reconsidered*, 18.

4. For the biographical assessments of Lincoln, see the "Bibliographical Essay" in this book. My own reading of Lincoln's life and meaning, particularly as it relates to his leadership, has been especially influenced by Phillip Shaw Paludan, *The Presidency of Abraham Lincoln* (Lawrence: University Press of Kansas, 1994); William E. Gienapp, *Abraham Lincoln and Civil War America: A Biography* (New York: Oxford University Press, 2002); Mark E. Neely Jr., *The Last Best Hope of Earth: Abraham Lincoln and the Promise of America* (Cambridge: Harvard University Press, 1993); Richard Carwardine, *Lincoln: A Life of Purpose and Power* (New York: Knopf, 2006); William Lee Miller, *President Lincoln: The Duty of a Statesman* (New York: Knopf, 2008); Allen C. Guelzo, *Abraham Lincoln: Redeemer President* (Grand Rapids, MI: Eerdmans, 1999); and with some reservations, David Herbert Donald, *Lincoln* (New York: Simon & Schuster, 1995); and James M. McPherson, *Tried by Fire: Abraham Lincoln as Commander in Chief* (New York: Penguin, 2008). For excellent state-of-the-field assessments, with important suggestions for new directions in scholarship, see the essays by Matthew Pinsker, Edward L. Ayers, Catherine Clinton, Michael F. Holt, Mark E. Neely Jr., and Douglas L. Wilson in "Lincoln Studies at the Bicentennial: A Round Table," *Journal of American History* 96 (2009): 417–61. Regarding the term "slave power," Lincoln and other Republicans meant the power of slaveholders able

to assert slavery's interest in westward expansion, in suppressing civil liberties, in silencing antislavery critics, and in dominating American political life.

5. Abraham Lincoln (hereafter AL) to Horace Greeley, August 22, 1862, in Roy P. Basler et al., eds., *The Collected Works of Abraham Lincoln*, 9 vols. (New Brunswick: Rutgers University Press, 1953), 5:388–89 (hereafter *Collected Works*).

6. AL to Orville H. Browning, September 22, 1861, in *Collected Works*, 4:532. On the importance of Kentucky and the border states in Lincoln's thinking and policy, see William C. Harris, *Lincoln and the Border States: Preserving the Union* (Lawrence: University Press of Kansas, 2011). For the long view on how the clashes of interests in the border states during the 1850s shaped the secession crisis, see Stanley Harrold, *Border War: Fighting over Slavery before the Civil War* (Chapel Hill: University of North Carolina Press, 2010).

7. On the appeal of the Union, see especially Elizabeth Varon, *Disunion: The Coming of the American Civil War, 1789–1859* (Chapel Hill: University of North Carolina Press, 2008), 1–2, 4–5. For the pervasiveness of the Union theme in popular thought, and as an animating force in resisting secession and then fighting to restore the Union, see Gary W. Gallagher, *The Union War* (Cambridge: Harvard University Press, 2011). For Americans' contested views of the Union, sectional interests, and ideas about rights and honor, see Shearer Davis Bowman, *At the Precipice: Americans North and South during the Secession Crisis* (Chapel Hill: University of North Carolina Press, 2010).

8. "First Inaugural Address—Final Text," March 4, 1861, in *Collected Works*, 4:263–71; "Annual Message to Congress," December 3, 1861, in ibid., 5:51, 53.

9. "Annual Message to Congress," December 1, 1862, in ibid., 5:537; "Gettysburg Address" (final text), November 19, 1863, in ibid., 7:23.

10. This and the following paragraphs on Lincoln and emancipation draw especially on Eric Foner, *The Fiery Trial: Abraham Lincoln and American Slavery* (New York: Norton, 2010), especially chaps. 6–9; Richard Striner, *Father Abraham: Lincoln's Relentless Struggle to End Slavery* (New York: Oxford University Press, 2006); George M. Fredrickson, *Big Enough to Be Inconsistent: Abraham Lincoln Confronts Slavery and Race* (Cambridge: Harvard University Press, 2008); Paludan, *Presidency of Abraham Lincoln*, 137–202; Miller, *President Lincoln*, 231–313; Allen C. Guelzo, *Lincoln's Emancipation Proclamation: The End of Slavery in America* (New York: Simon & Schuster, 2004); Frank J. Williams, "'Doing More' and 'Doing Less': The President and the Proclamation—Legally, Militarily, Politically," in Harold Holzer, Edna Greene Medford, and Frank J. Williams, *The Emancipation Proclamation: Three Views* (Baton Rouge: Louisiana State University Press, 2006), 43–82; Paul Finkelman, "Lincoln and the Preconditions for Emancipation: The Moral Grandeur of a Bill of Lading," in William A. Blair and Karen Fisher Younger, eds., *Lincoln's Proclamation: Emancipation Reconsidered* (Chapel Hill: University of North Carolina Press, 2009), 13–44; James Oakes, *The Radical and the Republican: Frederick Douglass, Abraham Lincoln, and the Triumph of Antislavery Politics* (New York: Norton, 2007); James Oakes, "Natural Rights, Citizenship Rights, and Black Rights: Another Look at Lincoln and Race," in Foner, ed., *Our Lincoln*, 109–34; Manisha Sinha, "Allies for Emancipation? Lincoln and Black Abolitionists," in ibid., 167–96; Paul D. Escott, *"What Shall We Do with the Negro?": Lincoln, White Racism, and Civil War America* (Charlottesville: University of

Virginia Press, 2009); Paul Finkelman, "The Civil War, Emancipation, and the Thirteenth Amendment: Understanding Who Freed the Slaves," in Alexander Tsesis, ed., *The Promises of Liberty: The History and Contemporary Relevance of the Thirteenth Amendment* (New York: Columbia University Press, 2010), 36–57; and James M. McPherson, "Who Freed the Slaves?," *Reconstruction* 2 (1994): 35–40.

11. "Annual Message to Congress," December 3, 1861, in *Collected Works*, 5:48–49.

12. See note 10 above for references for this and the next paragraphs. For a different view of Lincoln and colonization, arguing that Lincoln persisted in secret colonization schemes even after he issued the Emancipation Proclamation, see Phillip W. Magness and Sebastian N. Page, *Colonization after Emancipation: Lincoln and the Movement for Black Resettlement* (Columbia: University of Missouri Press, 2011).

13. Lincoln quoted in F[rancis] B[icknell] Carpenter, *The Inner Life of Abraham Lincoln: Six Months at the White House* (New York: Hurd & Houghton, 1872), 76.

14. On Lincoln and the Thirteenth Amendment, see Michael Vorenberg, *Final Freedom: The Civil War, the Abolition of Slavery, and the Thirteenth Amendment* (New York: Cambridge University Press, 2001). For the Lincoln quotation, see "Response to a Serenade," February 1, 1865, in *Collected Works*, 8:254. It is worth noting that constitutional amendments do not require a presidential signature.

15. On "positive liberty" as applied to Lincoln and the Republicans, see James M. McPherson, *Abraham Lincoln and the Second American Revolution* (New York: Oxford University Press, 1991), 43–64, 131–52; George P. Fletcher, *Our Secret Constitution: How Lincoln Redefined American Democracy* (New York: Oxford University Press, 2001); and John D. Fairfield, *The Public and Its Possibilities: Triumphs and Tragedies in the American City* (Philadelphia: Temple University Press, 2010), 45–52.

16. "Address at Sanitary Fair," April 18, 1864, in *Collected Works*, 7:301–2.

17. Vorenberg, *Final Freedom*, 176–210.

18. This and the following paragraphs on the policies, practices, and politics of arming black soldiers draw especially on John David Smith, "Let Us All Be Grateful That We Have Colored Soldiers That Will Fight," in John David Smith, ed., *Black Soldiers in Blue: African American Troops in the Civil War Era* (Chapel Hill: University of North Carolina Press, 2002), 1–77; Noah Trudeau, *Like Men of War: Black Troops in the Civil War, 1862–1865* (Boston: Little, Brown, 1998); and Joseph T. Glatthaar, *Forged in Battle: The Civil War Alliance of Black Soldiers and White Officers* (New York: Free Press, 1989). For the Lincoln statement on black soldiers, see "Address at Sanitary Fair," April 18, 1864, in *Collected Works*, 7:302.

19. AL to James C. Conkling, August 26, 1863, in *Collected Works*, 6:407, 409.

20. On Lincoln and Republican domestic policy, see especially Paludan, *Presidency of Abraham Lincoln*, 108–18; Heather Cox Richardson, *The Greatest Nation on Earth: Republican Economic Policies during the Civil War* (Cambridge: Harvard University Press, 1997); and Leonard P. Curry, *Blueprint for Modern America: Non-military Legislation of the First Civil War Congress* (Nashville: Vanderbilt University Press, 1968). On Lincoln's thinking about improvements, see especially Gabor Boritt, *Lincoln and the Economics of the American Dream* (Urbana: University of Illinois Press, 1994). Lincoln also did not deviate much

from prevailing thinking on Indian policy, which followed his western and pro-settlement inclinations. See David A. Nichols, *Lincoln and the Indians: Civil War Policy and Politics* (Columbia: University of Missouri Press, 1978).

21. Lincoln's first actions as president are detailed in Paludan, *Presidency of Abraham Lincoln*, 49–94; Miller, *President Lincoln*, 48–127; Russell McClintock, *Lincoln and the Decision for War: The Northern Response to Secession* (Chapel Hill: University of North Carolina Press, 2008), 227–74; and very critically in William Marvel, *Mr. Lincoln Goes to War* (Boston: Houghton Mifflin, 2006). On contemporary misreadings of conditions in 1861, see Emory M. Thomas, *The Dogs of War, 1861* (New York: Oxford University Press, 2011).

22. AL to Erastus Corning and Others, June 12, 1863, in *Collected Works*, 6:264. On Lincoln and civil liberties, see especially Mark E. Neely Jr., *The Fate of Liberty: Abraham Lincoln and Civil Liberties* (New York: Oxford University Press, 1991). Also instructive is Daniel Farber, *Lincoln's Constitution* (Chicago: University of Chicago Press, 2003), 143–75.

23. On Lincoln and Congress regarding management of war policy, see Bruce Tap, *Over Lincoln's Shoulder: The Committee on the Conduct of the War* (Lawrence: University Press of Kansas, 1998); Paludan, *Presidency of Abraham Lincoln*, 108–18; and the still useful T. Harry Williams, *Lincoln and the Radicals* (1941; Madison: University of Wisconsin Press, 1971).

24. This and the following paragraphs on Lincoln and Reconstruction draw principally on William C. Harris, *With Charity toward All: Lincoln and the Restoration of the Union* (Lexington: University Press of Kentucky, 1997); LaWanda Cox, *Lincoln and Black Freedom: A Study in Presidential Leadership* (Columbia: University of South Carolina Press, 1981); Brooks D. Simpson, *The Reconstruction Presidents* (Lawrence: University Press of Kansas, 1998), 9–64; Paludan, *Presidency of Abraham Lincoln*, 302–11; Michael Green, "Reconstructing the Nation, Reconstructing the Party: Postwar Republicans and the Evolution of a Party," in Paul A. Cimbala and Randall M. Miller, eds., *The Great Task Remaining before Us: Reconstruction as America's Continuing Civil War* (New York: Fordham University Press, 2010), 183–203; Herman Belz, *Reconstructing the Union: Theory and Policy during the Civil War* (Ithaca: Cornell University Press, 1969); Harold M. Hyman, *Lincoln's Reconstruction: Neither Failure of Vision nor Vision of Failure* (Fort Wayne, IN: Louis A. Warren Lincoln Library and Museum, 1980); and Michael Les Benedict, *A Compromise of Principle: Congressional Republicans and Reconstruction, 1863–1869* (New York: Norton, 1974). For the Lincoln quotation, see "Annual Message to Congress," December 8, 1863, in *Collected Works*, 7:52.

25. "Last Public Address," April 11, 1865, in *Collected Works*, 8:403.

26. Joseph Medill quoting Lincoln in H. I. Cleveland, "Booming the First Republican President: A Talk with Abraham Lincoln's Friend, the Late Joseph Medill," *Saturday Evening Post* 172 (August 5, 1899): 85.

27. On Lincoln's relationship with his cabinet, see Paludan, *Presidency of Abraham Lincoln*, 21–45, 168–81; Doris Kearns Goodwin, *Team of Rivals: The Political Genius of Abraham Lincoln* (New York: Simon & Schuster, 2005), 282–93, 312–19; and Burton J. Hendrick,

Lincoln's War Cabinet (Boston: Little, Brown, 1946). For a counterview to Goodwin, see Matthew Pinsker's chapter in this book.

28. On Lincoln's appointment of Chase, see James F. Simon, *Lincoln and Chief Justice Taney: Slavery, Secession, and the President's War Powers* (New York: Simon & Schuster, 2006), 267–68; Belz, *Reconstructing the Union*, 246–47; and Paludan, *Presidency of Abraham Lincoln*, 302–3. On Lincoln's relationship with the Supreme Court, see Brian McGinty, *Lincoln and the Court* (Cambridge: Harvard University Press, 2008); and for Lincoln's thinking about and working within the constitutional framework, see Mark E. Neely Jr., *Lincoln and the Triumph of the Nation: Constitutional Conflict in the American Civil War* (Chapel Hill: University of North Carolina Press, 2011).

29. See note 27 above for this paragraph and the next.

30. On the character and limits of Lincoln's friendships, see David Herbert Donald, *"We Are Lincoln Men": Abraham Lincoln and His Friends* (New York: Simon & Schuster, 2003).

31. Matthew Pinsker, *Lincoln's Sanctuary: Abraham Lincoln and the Soldiers' Home* (New York: Oxford University Press, 2003).

32. "Eulogy on Henry Clay," July 6, 1852, in *Collected Works*, 2:126.

33. On Lincoln and politics, see Miller, *Lincoln's Virtues*, 92–115; Donald, *Lincoln*; Michael S. Green, *Freedom, Union, and Power: Lincoln and His Party during the Civil War* (New York: Fordham University Press, 2004); Richard Carwardine, "'A Party Man Who Did Not Believe in Any Man Who Was Not': Abraham Lincoln, the Republican Party, and the Union," in William Cooper Jr. and John M. McCardell Jr., eds., *In the Cause of Liberty: How the Civil War Redefined American Ideals* (Baton Rouge: Louisiana State University Press, 2009), 40–62; Richard Hofstadter, *The American Political Tradition and Those Who Made It* (1948; New York: Vintage, 1973), 119–73; and Richard Norton Smith, *Abraham Lincoln and the Triumph of Politics* (Gettysburg: Gettysburg College, 2007). On the political climate in which Lincoln operated, and relationships within the Republican Party, see Mark E. Neely Jr., *The Union Divided: Party Conflict in the Civil War North* (Cambridge: Harvard University Press, 2002); and Adam I. P. Smith, *No Party Now: Politics in the Civil War North* (New York: Oxford University Press, 2006).

34. On the 1864 election, in addition to the references in note 33 above, see especially John C. Waugh, *Reelecting Lincoln: The Battle for the 1864 Presidency* (New York: Crown, 1997); and Matthew Pinsker's chapter in this volume.

35. "Response to a Serenade," November 10, 1864, in *Collected Works*, 8:101.

36. David M. Potter, "Civil War," in C. Vann Woodward, ed., *The Comparative Approach to American History* (New York: Basic, 1968), 141–44. On Lincoln's and the war's place in reshaping the world, see also James M. McPherson, "'For a Vast Future Also': Lincoln and the Millennium," in Susan-Mary Grant and Peter J. Parish, eds., *Legacy of Disunion: The Enduring Significance of the American Civil War* (Baton Rouge: Louisiana State University Press, 2003), 134–47; and Michael Knox Beran, *Forge of Empires, 1861–1871: Three Revolutionary Statesmen and the World They Made* (New York: Free Press, 2007), on Lincoln, Tsar Alexander II, and Otto von Bismarck and nation building. On political

courage, see Allan Nevins's comments in his preface to John F. Kennedy, *Profiles in Courage* (New York: Harper, 1955), xix–xx.

37. This and the following paragraphs on Lincoln as commander in chief draw on McPherson, *Tried by War*; with some reservations, Geoffrey Perret, *Lincoln's War: The Untold Story of America's Greatest President as Commander in Chief* (New York: Random House, 2004); Gabor S. Boritt, ed., *Lincoln, the War President: The Gettysburg Lectures* (New York: Oxford University Press, 1992); Gabor S. Boritt, ed., *Lincoln's Generals* (New York: Oxford University Press, 1994); Herman Hattaway and Archer Jones, *How the North Won: A Military History of the Civil War* (Urbana: University of Illinois Press, 1983); Russell F. Weigley, *A Great Civil War: A Military and Political History, 1861–1865* (Bloomington: Indiana University Press, 2000); Donald Stoker, *The Grand Design: Strategy and the U.S. Civil War* (New York: Oxford University Press, 2010); and T. Harry Williams, *Lincoln and His Generals* (New York: Knopf, 1952). For an assessment of Lincoln and his "political generals" that emphasizes their overall value politically and even as military men, see David Work, *Lincoln's Political Generals* (Urbana: University of Illinois Press, 2009); and for an argument that Lincoln adroitly managed his generals, see Chester G. Hearn, *Lincoln, the Cabinet, and the Generals* (Baton Rouge: Louisiana State University Press, 2010).

38. "Speech in U.S. House of Representatives on the Presidential Question," July 27, 1848, in *Collected Works*, 1:510.

39. "Annual Message to Congress," December 3, 1861, in ibid., 5:51.

40. AL to Don C. Buell, January 13, 1862, in ibid., 5:98.

41. AL to Andrew H. Foote, January 23, 1862, in ibid., 5:108.

42. AL to George B. McClellan, April 9, 1862, in ibid., 5:184–85.

43. On Lincoln's relationship with men in the ranks, see especially William C. Davis, *Lincoln's Men: How President Lincoln Became Father to an Army and a Nation* (New York: Free Press, 1999).

44. AL to George B. McClellan, May 1, 1862, in *Collected Works*, 5:203; and AL to McClellan, October 13, 1862, in ibid., 5:460–61.

45. AL to Joseph Hooker, January 26, 1863, in ibid., 6:78–79.

46. Lincoln quoted in Don E. Fehrenbacher and Virginia Fehrenbacher, eds., *Recollected Words of Abraham Lincoln* (Stanford: Stanford University Press, 1996), 292.

47. AL to Ulysses S. Grant, July 13, 1863, in *Collected Works*, 6:326. On his confidence in Grant, see, for example, AL to Ulysses S. Grant, April 30, 1864, in ibid., 7:324.

48. AL to Henry W. Halleck, September 19, 1863, in ibid., 6:466–67.

49. On the shift to hard war, see especially Mark Grimsley, *The Hard Hand of War: Union Military Policy toward Southern Civilians, 1861–1865* (Cambridge: Cambridge University Press, 1995), 142–204. On Lincoln's thinking about the legal and moral implications of such a policy, see Burrus M. Carnahan, *Lincoln on Trial: Southern Civilians and the Law of War* (Lexington: University Press of Kentucky, 2010); and for a more condemnatory view, see Harry S. Stout, *Upon the Altar of the Nation: A Moral History of the Civil War* (New York: Viking, 2006).

50. Henry W. Halleck to Ulysses S. Grant, February 17, 1864, in *War of the Rebellion: A Compilation of the Official Records of the Union and Confederate Armies*, 70 volumes in

128 serials (Washington, DC: Government Printing Office, 1880–1901), ser. 1, vol. 32, pt. 2, p. 412; and AL to Ulysses S. Grant, August 17, 1864, in *Collected Works*, 7:499.

51. On Lincoln's use of photography and control over his image, see Harold Holzer, "The Campaign of 1860: Cooper Union, Mathew Brady, and the Campaign of Words and Images," in John W. Simon, Harold Holzer, and Dawn Vogel, eds., *Lincoln Revisited: New Insights from the Lincoln Forum* (New York: Fordham University Press, 2007), 57–80; Harold Holzer, "Visualizing Lincoln: Abraham Lincoln as Student, Subject, and Patron of the Visual Arts," in Foner, ed., *Our Lincoln*, 80–106; and Harold Holzer, Gabor S. Boritt, and Mark E. Neely Jr., *The Lincoln Image: Abraham Lincoln and the Popular Print* (New York: Scribner, 1984).

52. On Lincoln and his family, compare Stephen Berry, *House of Abraham: Lincoln and the Todds, a Family Divided by War* (New York: HarperCollins, 2007); Daniel Epstein, *The Lincolns: Portrait of a Marriage* (New York: Ballantine, 2009); Jerrold M. Packard, *The Lincolns in the White House: Four Years That Shattered a Family* (New York: St. Martin's Griffin, 2005); Catherine Clinton, *Mrs. Lincoln: A Life* (New York: HarperCollins, 2009); and Jean H. Baker, *Mary Todd Lincoln: A Biography* (New York: Norton, 1987), especially 130–207. On Lincoln's unhitching himself from southern ties, see Stephen Berry, "'I Always Thought "Dixie" One of the Best Tunes I Ever Heard': Lincoln's Claims on the South and the South's Claims on Lincoln," *Journal of the Historical Society* 9 (2009): 325–39; and for a perceptive review of Lincoln's Kentucky connections and concerns, see John David Smith, "'Gentlemen, I Too Am a Kentuckian': Abraham Lincoln, the Lincoln Bicentennial, and Lincoln's Kentucky in Recent Scholarship," *Register of the Kentucky Historical Society* 106 (2008): 433–70.

53. Donald, *Lincoln*, 581.

54. "Second Lecture on Discoveries and Inventions," [February 11, 1859], in *Collected Works*, 3:360.

55. "Meditation on the Divine Will," [September 2, 1862?], in ibid., 5:403–4.

56. On Lincoln and his evolving thinking on religion, Providence, history, America, and the war, see especially Guelzo, *Abraham Lincoln*, 312–14, 318–25, 439–48; Carwardine, *Lincoln*, 32–44, 221–28; Richard Carwardine, "Lincoln's Religion," in Foner, ed., *Our Lincoln*, 223–48; Douglas L. Wilson, *Lincoln's Sword: The Presidency and the Power of Words* (New York: Knopf, 2006), 250–63; Miller, *Lincoln's Virtues*, 82–91, 295–96; Wayne C. Temple, *Abraham Lincoln: From Skeptic to Prophet* (Mahomet, IL: Mayhaven, 1995); Grant Havers, *Lincoln and the Politics of Christian Love* (Columbia: University of Missouri Press, 2009); and for a larger context, George Rable, *God's Almost Chosen Peoples: A Religious History of the American Civil War* (Chapel Hill: University of North Carolina Press, 2010).

57. This and the following paragraphs on Lincoln's writing—its sources, style, and substance—draw on Fred Kaplan, *Lincoln: The Biography of a Writer* (New York: HarperCollins, 2008); Wilson, *Lincoln's Sword*; Ronald C. White Jr., *The Eloquent President: A Portrait of Lincoln through His Words* (New York: Random House, 2005); Harold Holzer, *Lincoln at Cooper Union: The Speech That Made Abraham Lincoln President* (New York: Simon & Schuster, 2004); Andrew Delbanco, "Lincoln's Sacramental Language," in Foner,

ed., *Our Lincoln*, 199–222; and Robert Bray, *Reading with Lincoln* (Carbondale: Southern Illinois University Press, 2010).

58. "Gettysburg Address" (final text), November 19, 1863, in *Collected Works*, 7:23.

59. On Stanton's words and the larger meaning of Lincoln they entailed—whether "Now he belongs to the ages" or "Now he belongs to the angels"—see Adam Gopnik, "Angels and Ages: Lincoln's Language and Its Legacy," *New Yorker*, May 28, 2007, 31–37.

2. Sowing the Wind and Reaping the Whirlwind: Abraham Lincoln as a War President / Gregory J. W. Urwin

1. Merrill D. Peterson discusses the evolution of the Lincoln image in *Lincoln in American Memory* (New York: Oxford University Press, 1994).

2. Lance J. Herdegen, *Those Damned Black Hats! The Iron Brigade in the Gettysburg Campaign* (New York: Savas Beatie, 2008), 49–50. See also William C. Davis, *Lincoln's Men: How President Lincoln Became Father to an Army and a Nation* (New York: Free Press, 1999).

3. *Brief Historical Sketch of the Cuyahoga County Soldiers' and Sailors' Monument* (1896; Cleveland: Monument Commissioners, 1965), 10–24, 31–32.

4. T. Harry Williams, *The History of American Wars from 1745 to 1918* (Baton Rouge: Louisiana State University Press, 1981), 248.

5. Abraham Lincoln (hereafter AL), "Speech in Congress," July 27, 1848, in John G. Nicolay and John Hay, eds., *Complete Works of Abraham Lincoln*, 12 vols. (Harrogate: Lincoln Memorial University, 1894) 12:60; and Williams, *History of American Wars*, 248. For T. Harry Williams's full take on Lincoln as a war president, see *Lincoln and His Generals* (New York: Knopf, 1952).

6. For a plausible psychological interpretation of how Lincoln viewed the Union, see Charles B. Strozier, *Lincoln's Quest for Union: Public and Private Meanings* (1982; Urbana: University of Illinois Press, 1987).

7. AL, "Message to Congress in Special Session," July 4, 1861, in Roy P. Basler et al., eds., *The Collected Works of Abraham Lincoln*, 9 vols. (New Brunswick: Rutgers University Press, 1953–55), 4:438 (hereafter *Collected Works*).

8. AL, "Annual Message to Congress," December 1, 1862, in ibid., 5:537.

9. Herman Hattaway and Archer Jones, *How the North Won: A Military History of the Civil War* (Urbana: University of Illinois Press, 1983), 5; Russell F. Weigley, *A Great Civil War: A Military and Political History, 1861–1865* (Bloomington: Indiana University Press, 2000), 90–92.

10. Mark E. Neely Jr., *The Fate of Liberty: Abraham Lincoln and Civil Liberties* (New York: Oxford University Press, 1991), 4–138, 160–209.

11. Ibid., 137–38.

12. AL, "Message to Congress in Special Session," July 4, 1861, in *Collected Works*, 4:430.

13. Edward Younger, ed., *Inside the Confederate Government: The Diary of Robert Garlick Hill Kean, Head of the Bureau of War* (New York: Oxford University Press, 1957), 101.

14. Lincoln also had to take care to provide such European powers as Great Britain and France with no pretext for recognizing Confederate independence. James M. McPherson, *Battle Cry of Freedom: The Civil War Era* (New York: Oxford University Press, 1988), 274, 313, 355; Weigley, *Great Civil War*, 24, 56–57.

15. Williams, *History of American Wars*, 248–49.

16. AL to Brigadier General Don Carlos Buell, January 13, 1862, in Paul M. Engle and Earl Schenck Miers, eds., *The Living Lincoln: The Man and His Times, in His Own Words* (1955; New York: Barnes and Noble, 1992), 459–60. Lincoln also had a copy of this letter sent to Major General Henry Wager Halleck.

17. Williams, *History of American Wars*, 248–53.

18. Ibid., 321.

19. AL to A. G. Hodges, April 4, 1864, in *Collected Works*, 7:282.

20. Williams, *History of American Wars*, 211–13.

21. AL to Lyman Trumbull, December, 10, 1860, in Don E. Fehrenbacher, ed., *Lincoln: Speeches and Writings*, 2 vols. (New York: Library of America, 1989), 2:190.

22. The effect the Civil War's enormous death toll had on Americans of that era receives perceptive treatment in Drew Gilpin Faust, *This Republic of Suffering: Death and the American Civil War* (New York: Knopf, 2008).

23. Hattaway and Jones, *How the North Won*, 5–6.

24. See McPherson's *Battle Cry of Freedom*, 276–84; and *Ordeal by Fire: The Civil War and Reconstruction* (New York: Knopf, 1982), 149–51.

25. Earl J. Hess, "Politics, Ethnicity, and Military Operations: Franz Siegel," and Mark Grimsley, "'A Lack of Confidence': Benjamin F. Butler," both in Steven E. Woodworth, ed., *Grant's Lieutenants: From Chattanooga to Appomattox* (Lawrence: University Press of Kansas, 2008), 84–132. See also James G. Hollandsworth Jr., *Pretense of Glory: The Life of General Nathaniel P. Banks* (Baton Rouge: Louisiana State University Press, 1998); and Stephen D. Engle, *Yankee Dutchman: The Life of Franz Sigel* (Fayetteville: University of Arkansas Press, 1993).

26. Early's operations and their aftermath are ably covered in Frank E. Vandiver, *Jubal's Raid: General Early's Famous Attack on Washington in 1864* (New York: McGraw-Hill, 1960); and Jeffry D. Wert, *From Winchester to Cedar Creek: The Shenandoah Campaign of 1864* (Mechanicsburg, PA: Stackpole, 1997).

27. Hattaway and Jones, *How the North Won*, 485–96, 516–22. See also Ludwell H. Johnson, *Red River Campaign: Politics & Cotton in the Civil War* (1958; Kent: Kent State University Press, 1993); Chester G. Hearn, *Mobile Bay and the Mobile Campaign* (Jefferson, NC: McFarland, 1993); T. Michael Parrish, *Richard Taylor, Soldier Prince of Dixie* (Chapel Hill: University of North Carolina Press, 1992); Jeffery S. Prushankin, *A Crisis in Confederate Command: Edmund Kirby Smith, Richard Taylor, and the Army of the Trans-Mississippi* (Baton Rouge: Louisiana State University Press, 2005); and A. F. Sperry, *History of the 33d Iowa Infantry Volunteer Regiment 1863–6*, Gregory J. W. Urwin and Cathy Kunzinger Urwin, eds. (Fayetteville: University of Arkansas Press, 1999).

28. The best recent biography of McClellan is Stephen W. Sears, *George B. McClellan: The Young Napoleon* (New York: Ticknor & Fields, 1988). Also useful is Ethan J. Rafuse,

McClellan's War: The Failure of Moderation in the Struggle for the Union (Bloomington: Indiana University Press, 2005). For an unusually sympathetic interpretation of McClellan's relations with Lincoln and other Union politicians, see Russel H. Beatie, *McClellan Takes Command, September 1861–February 1862, vol. 2 of Army of the Potomac* (Cambridge, MA: Da Capo, 2004).

29. William B. Skelton, in *An American Profession of Arms: The Army Officer Corps, 1784–1861* (Lawrence: University Press of Kansas, 1992), alerted historians to the significant strides that professionalization made in the antebellum army. Skelton's pioneering work is richly complemented by Richard N. Grippaldi, "Birth of the U. S. Cavalry: The Regiment of Dragoons, Military Professionalism, and Peacekeeping along the Permanent Indian Frontier, 1833–1836" (PhD diss., Temple University, 2011). A superb campaign study that explains how the War of 1812 became an important impetus in this process is Richard V. Barbuto, *Niagara, 1814: America Invades Canada* (Lawrence: University Press of Kansas, 2000).

30. John F. Marszalek, *Commander of All Lincoln's Armies: A Life of General Henry W. Halleck* (Cambridge: Harvard University Press, 2004), 21.

31. John M. Carroll, ed., *Custer in the Civil War: His Unfinished Memoirs* (San Rafael, CA: Presidio Press, 1977), 121–22. For more on Custer in the Civil War and beyond, see Gregory J. W. Urwin, "Custer: The Civil War Years," in Paul A. Hutton, ed., *The Custer Reader* (Lincoln: University of Nebraska Press, 1992), 7–32; Robert M. Utley, *Cavalier in Buckskin: George Armstrong Custer and the Western Military Frontier* (Norman: University of Oklahoma Press, 1988); and Jeffry D. Wert, *Custer: The Controversial Life of George Armstrong Custer* (New York: Simon & Schuster, 1996).

32. Marszalek, *Commander of All Lincoln's Armies*, 48–111, 128–226.

33. James M. McPherson assesses the impact of the Emancipation Proclamation in *Crossroads of Freedom: Antietam* (New York: Oxford University Press, 2002), 138–46.

34. *Christian Recorder* (Philadelphia), June 25, 1864. See also Joseph T. Glatthaar, *Forged in Battle: The Civil War Alliance of Black Soldiers and White Officers* (New York: Free Press, 1999), 2–3, 71, 79–80, 145, 153, 227–30.

35. Glatthaar, *Forged in Battle*, 205. For Lincoln's fidelity to the Union's black soldiers and his refusal to temporize on emancipation during the 1864 presidential race, see David E. Long, *The Jewel of Liberty: Abraham Lincoln's Re-election and the End of Slavery* (Mechanicsburg, PA: Stackpole, 1994). Long does admit that the prospect of not being reelected caused Lincoln to briefly waver behind the scenes in his commitment to emancipation in late August 1864. The beleaguered president also toyed with the idea of inviting Confederate leaders to a peace conference. Luckily for the Union cause, a mounting tide of military victories boosted northern morale and Lincoln held firm to his basic war goals—reunion and the death of slavery.

36. George S. Burkhardt, *Confederate Rage, Yankee Wrath: No Quarter in the Civil War* (Carbondale: Southern Illinois University Press, 2007), 12, 27–42.

37. Thomas Jefferson to John Holmes, April 20, 1822, Thomas Jefferson Papers, Manuscript Division, Library of Congress, Washington; Thomas Jefferson to Mrs. Sigourney, July 18, 1824, in "Original Documents: Three Unpublished Family Letters," *Magazine of*

American History 21 (May 1889): 431; Gregory J. W. Urwin, "Introduction: Warfare, Race, and the Civil War in American Memory," in Gregory J. W. Urwin, ed., *Black Flag over Dixie: Racial Atrocities and Reprisals in the Civil War* (Carbondale: Southern Illinois University Press, 2004), 5–6; James C. Bates to "Dear Sister," June 16, 1862, in Richard Lowe, ed., *A Texas Cavalry Officer's Civil War: The Diary and Letters of James C. Bates* (Baton Rouge: Louisiana State University Press, 1999), 119–20; Bertram Wyatt-Brown, *Southern Honor: Ethics and Behavior in the Old South* (New York: Oxford University Press, 1983), 402–61; and James Oakes, *The Ruling Race: A History of the Old South* (New York: Vintage, 1983), 22–24, 28–29, 49, 179–90, 218–19.

38. U.S. Congress, House, *Register of Debates*, 23rd Cong., 2nd sess., February 16, 1835, vol. 11, pt. 2, col. 1399.

39. Steven A. Channing made this case effectively in *Crisis of Fear: Secession in South Carolina* (1970; New York: Norton, 1974).

40. For a particularly vivid examination of the intense fear and outrage that the British use of Indian warriors aroused among their American foes during the War of 1812, see Alan Taylor, *The Civil War of 1812: American Citizens, British Subjects, Irish Rebels, & Indian Allies* (New York: Knopf, 2010), 125–27, 158–59, 162–73, 203–14, 225–32, 240–42, 258–61, 426–28. John F. Luzader, *Saratoga: A Military History of the Decisive Campaign of the American Revolution* (New York: Savas Beatie, 2008), recounts how Indian depredations incensed Americans and intensified resistance against British Lieutenant General John Burgoyne's ill-fated attempt to march from Canada to Albany, New York, in 1777. Rich insights regarding the ambivalence that many British politicians felt over employing Indian allies can be found in Jim Piecuch, *Three Peoples, One King: Loyalists, Indians, and Slaves in the Revolutionary South, 1775–1782* (Columbia: University of South Carolina Press, 2008). On southern fears during the Civil War, see Burkhardt, *Confederate Rage, Yankee Wrath*, 27–29; and James M. McPherson, *Abraham Lincoln and the Second American Revolution* (New York: Oxford University Press, 1991), 35.

41. Mark Grimsley, *The Hard Hand of War: Union Military Policy toward Southern Civilians* (Cambridge: Cambridge University Press, 1995), 133; "Domestic Intelligence," *Harper's Weekly*, January 31, 1863, 67.

42. *Washington Telegraph*, June 8, 1864; *Arkansas Gazette*, October 11, 1862; *True Democrat*, April 22, 1863.

43. Mark Grimsley, "'A Very Long Shadow': Race, Atrocity, and the American Civil War," in Urwin, ed., *Black Flag over Dixie*, 231–41; Mark K. Christ, "Who Wrote the Poison Spring Letter," in Mark K. Christ, ed., *"All Cut to Pieces and Gone to Hell": The Civil War, Race Relations, and the Battle of Poison Spring* (Little Rock: August House, 2003), 100.

44. *Washington Telegraph*, June 8, 1864. A complete description of this battle and the war crimes committed there can be found in Gregory J. W. Urwin, "Poison Spring and Jenkins Ferry: Racial Atrocities during the Camden Expedition," in Christ, ed., *All Cut to Pieces*, 107–28. See also Gregory J. W. Urwin, "'We Cannot Treat Negroes . . . as Prisoners of War': Racial Atrocities and Reprisals in Civil War Arkansas," in Urwin, ed., *Black Flag over Dixie*, 132–52. Detailed examinations of the Civil War's more famous racial war crimes at Fort Pillow, Tennessee, and the Battle of the Crater at Petersburg, Virginia, can be found

in John Cimprich, *Fort Pillow, a Civil War Massacre, and Public Memory* (Baton Rouge: Louisiana State University Press, 2005); Richard L. Fuchs, *An Unerring Fire: The Massacre at Fort Pillow* (Rutherford: Fairleigh Dickinson University Press, 1994); Gregory J. Malacusco, *The Fort Pillow Massacre: The Reason Why* (New York: Vantage, 1989); John Gauss, *Black Flag! Black Flag! The Battle of Fort Pillow* (Lanham, MD: University Press of America, 2003); Andrew Ward, *River Run Red: The Fort Pillow Massacre in the American Civil War* (New York: Viking, 2005); Brian Steel Wills, *A Battle from the Start: The Life of Nathan Bedford Forrest* (New York: HarperCollins, 1992); Richard Slotkin, *No Quarter: The Battle of the Crater, 1864* (New York: Random House, 2009); Michael A. Cavanaugh and William Marvel, *The Petersburg Campaign: The Battle of the Crater, "The Horrid Pit," June 25–August 6, 1864* (Lynchburg, VA: H. E. Howard, 1989); and Earl J. Hess, *Into the Crater: The Mine Attack at Petersburg* (Columbia: University of South Carolina Press, 2010).

45. Anonymous to "Dear Sallie," April 20, 1864, Spence Family Collection, Old State House Museum, Little Rock; William Blain to "Dear Wife," May 17, 1864, in Dolly Bottens, comp., *Rouse Stevens Ancestry & Allied Families* (Carthage, MO: privately printed, 1970), 108B; Glatthaar, *Forged in Battle*, 157–58; Urwin, "Poison Spring and Jenkins Ferry," 128–33.

46. William E. Gienapp, *Abraham Lincoln and Civil War America* (New York: Oxford University Press, 2002), 52, 64–65, 111–12, 129; Burkhardt, *Confederate Rage, Yankee Wrath*, 2–3, 77–79, 91–92, 243–44; Richard J. Carwardine, *Lincoln* (Harlow, Essex: Pearson/Longman, 2003), 22–23, 75–76, 211; Derek W. Frisby, "'Remember Fort Pillow!': Politics, Atrocity Propaganda, and the Evolution of Hard War," in Urwin, ed., *Black Flag over Dixie*, 121. Daniel E. Sutherland reveals the willingness of many Confederates to greet Union armies with merciless and unremitting guerrilla warfare from the war's opening guns in *A Savage Conflict: The Decisive Role of Guerrillas in the American Civil War* (Chapel Hill: University of North Carolina Press, 2009). See also Clay Mountcastle, *Punitive War: Confederate Guerrillas and Union Reprisals* (Lawrence: University Press of Kansas, 2009).

47. The most comprehensive history of Civil War POW policy, which is equally condemnatory in its treatment of both sides, is Charles W. Sanders Jr., *While in the Hands of the Enemy: Military Prisons of the Civil War* (Baton Rouge: Louisiana State University Press, 2005).

48. An anthology devoted to the same theme as this chapter is Gabor S. Boritt, ed., *Lincoln, the War President: The Gettysburg Lectures* (New York: Oxford University Press, 1992). The latest word on the subject is James M. McPherson, *Tried by War: Abraham Lincoln as Commander in Chief* (New York: Penguin, 2008).

49. Walt Whitman, "Specimen Days (1882–83)," in Louis P. Masur, ed., *". . . The Real War Will Never Get into the Books": Selections from Writers during the Civil War* (New York: Oxford University Press, 1993), 281.

3. Seeing Lincoln's Blind Memorandum / Matthew Pinsker

1. "Memorandum Concerning His Probable Failure of Re-election," August 23, 1864, in Roy P. Basler et al., eds., *The Collected Works of Abraham Lincoln*, 9 vols. (New Brunswick:

Rutgers University Press, 1953): 7:514 (hereafter *Collected Works*); Hay diary entry, November 11, 1864, in Michael Burlingame and John R. Turner Ettlinger, eds., *Inside Lincoln's White House: The Complete Civil War Diary of John Hay* (Carbondale: Southern Illinois University Press, 1997), 247–48.

2. Hay diary entry, November 11, 1864, in Burlingame and Ettlinger, eds., *Inside Lincoln's White House*, 247–48.

3. Gideon Welles, "The Opposition to Lincoln in 1864," *Atlantic Monthly* 41 (March 1878): 367.

4. John Hay to John G. Nicolay, February 27, 1878, in William Roscoe Thayer, *John Hay: American Statesman*, 2 vols. (New York: Harper & Bros., 1915), 2:21–22.

5. John G. Nicolay and John Hay, *Abraham Lincoln: A History*, 10 vols. (New York: Century, 1890), 9:249–51.

6. "Memorandum Concerning His Probable Failure of Re-election," in *Collected Works*, 7:514–15n.

7. James G. Randall and Richard N. Current, *Lincoln the President: Last Full Measure* (New York: Dodd, Mead, 1955), 215–16.

8. Mark E. Neely Jr., "The Lincoln Theme since Randall's Call: The Promises and Perils of Professionalism," *Journal of the Abraham Lincoln Association* 1 (1979): 18–19. Neely further popularized the use of the term "blind memorandum" when he incorporated the label as an entry for his important reference work *The Abraham Lincoln Encyclopedia* (New York: McGraw-Hill, 1982).

9. James M. McPherson, *Battle Cry of Freedom: The Civil War Era* (New York: Oxford University Press, 1988), 771. Although McPherson used quotation marks for "blind memorandum," he did not cite Neely and yet none of the sources in his relevant footnote employed this phrase—further evidence for how quickly the term had achieved popularity.

10. October 17, 1861, in Burlingame and Ettlinger, eds., *Inside Lincoln's White House*, 26.

11. David Donald, *Lincoln's Herndon* (1948; New York: Da Capo, 1989), 153.

12. Maurice Cowling, *1867: Disraeli, Gladstone, and Revolution* (Cambridge: Cambridge University Press, 1967), 3. During the 1970s, Cowling led what has been called the "high politics" school in mid-Victorian history, a movement that emphasized ambition and power as leading factors in political decision making, and thick narrative as the most suitable forum for comprehending political action. Typical of the high political approach were monographs such as Andrew Jones, *The Politics of Reform, 1884* (Cambridge: Cambridge University Press, 1972); and A. B. Cooke and John Vincent, *The Governing Passion: Cabinet Government and Party Politics in Britain, 1885–86* (Brighton, Eng.: Harvester, 1974). For a spirited defense of the approach, see Andrew Jones, "Where 'Governing Is the Use of Words,'" *Historical Journal* 19 (1976): 251–56. For much more skeptical critiques, see Lawrence Goldman, "The Social Science Association, 1857–1886: A Context for Mid-Victorian Liberalism," *English Historical Review* 101 (January 1986): 95–134; and Richard Brent, "Butterfield's Tories: 'High Politics' and the Writing of Modern British Political History," *Historical Journal* 30 (December 1987): 943–54.

13. David E. Long, *The Jewel of Liberty: Abraham Lincoln's Re-election and the End of Slavery* (1994; New York: Da Capo, 1997), 252. For a provocative analysis of Union politi-

cal movements, see Michael Holt, "Abraham Lincoln and the Politics of Union," in John L. Thomas, ed., *Abraham Lincoln and the American Political Tradition* (Amherst: University of Massachusetts Press, 1986). See also Mark E. Neely Jr.'s *The Last Best Hope of Earth: Abraham Lincoln and the Promise of America* (Cambridge: Harvard University Press, 1993), 159–82; and *The Union Divided: Political Conflict in the Civil War North* (Cambridge: Harvard University Press, 2002).

14. "Response to a Serenade," November 10, 1864, in *Collected Works*, 8:101.

15. There are now three solid monographs available on the campaign. William Frank Zornow, *Lincoln and the Party Divided* (Norman: University of Oklahoma Press, 1954), remains the most complete political narrative, despite some outdated interpretations of the Radical Republicans, whom the author labels the "Unconditionals" and whom he generally treats with disdain (p. 3). David Long, *Jewel of Liberty*, sometimes strains to argue that the election was "the most important one in history" (p. 265), but this account nevertheless presents the most sophisticated analysis of the campaign's issues. John C. Waugh, in *Reelecting Lincoln: The Battle for the 1864 Presidency* (New York: Crown, 1997), describes himself as a "historical reporter" (p. x) rather than a historian, and not coincidentally offers the most engaging, but not always the most nuanced, narrative. Despite the various merits of these monographs, the most reliable treatment of the contest comes from David Herbert Donald, *Lincoln* (New York: Simon & Schuster, 1995); see especially chaps. 18–19.

16. Robinson had written that the president's refusal to negotiate "without the abandonment of slavery . . . puts the whole war question on a new basis, and takes us War Democrats clear off our feet, leaving us no ground to stand upon." Quoted in *Collected Works*, 7:501n. Earl Schenck Miers, ed., *Lincoln Day by Day: A Chronology, 1809–1865* (Dayton, OH: Morningside, 1991), 279. Out of three principal monographs on the 1864 contest, none takes note of the juxtaposition of the Randall and Douglass meetings; see Long, *Jewel of Liberty*, 189–90; and Waugh, *Reelecting Lincoln*, 267. William Zornow does not even cover the episode in *Lincoln and the Party Divided*. David Donald, however, does include at least some material from both meetings; see *Lincoln*, 526–27. For the documents in question, see "To Whom It May Concern," July 18, 1864, in *Collected Works*, 7:451; and Abraham Lincoln to Charles D. Robinson, August 17, 1864, in *Collected Works*, 7:499–502.

17. Joseph T. Mills, a federal judge from Wisconsin, joined Randall. William P. Dole, an Indian Affairs commissioner, was also present after the meeting began. Mills took notes, which were later published in various newspapers and magazines, including *Harper's Weekly*. Much of the text from his account has been included in *Collected Works*, 7:506–8. For a more complete background on the meeting, see Matthew Pinsker, *Lincoln's Sanctuary: Abraham Lincoln and the Soldiers' Home* (New York: Oxford University Press, 2003), 157–62.

18. There are two versions of Lincoln's draft reply to Robinson in his papers. See Abraham Lincoln to Charles D. Robinson, August 17, 1864 [pencil draft], and Abraham Lincoln to Charles D. Robinson, [August 1864], in Abraham Lincoln Papers, Library of Congress, Washington.

19. On the subject of Lincoln's habit of holding back angry letters, see Doris Kearns Goodwin, *Team of Rivals: The Political Genius of Abraham Lincoln* (New York: Simon & Schuster, 1995), 536.

20. Frederick Douglass to Theodore Tilton, October 15, 1864, in Philip S. Foner, ed., *The Life and Writings of Frederick Douglass*, 5 vols. (New York: International, 1975): 3:423–24.

21. Quoted in Robert S. Harper, *Lincoln and the Press* (New York: McGraw-Hill, 1951), 309.

22. Christopher N. Breiseth, "Lincoln and Frederick Douglass: Another Debate," *Journal of the Illinois Historical Society* 68 (February 1975): 19.

23. Frederick Douglass to Theodore Tilton, October 15, 1864, in Foner, ed., *Life and Writings of Frederick Douglass*, 3:423.

24. Ibid.

25. Frederick Douglass to Abraham Lincoln August 29, 1864, Abraham Lincoln Papers, Library of Congress, Washington. See also Breiseth, "Lincoln and Frederick Douglass," 20; and William S. McFeely, *Frederick Douglass* (New York: Norton, 1991), 230.

26. Abraham Lincoln to Charles T. Robinson, August 17, 1864, in *Collected Works*, 7:499–502; interview with Alexander W. Randall and Joseph T. Mills, August 19, 1864, in *Collected Works*, 7:507.

27. Thurlow Weed to William Henry Seward, August 22, 1864, quoted in Nicolay and Hay, *Abraham Lincoln*, 9:250. Henry M. Raymond to Abraham Lincoln, August 22, 1864, Abraham Lincoln Papers, Library of Congress, Washington.

28. From J. K. Herbert to Benjamin Butler, August 6, 1864, and August 11, 1864, and N. G. Upham to Benjamin Butler, August 12, 1864, quoted in Jesse A. Marshall, ed., *Private and Official Correspondence of General Benjamin F. Butler during the Period of the Civil War*, 5 vols. (Norwood, MA: Plimpton, 1917), 5:35–37. See also Donald, *Lincoln*, 529.

29. Quoted in Francis F. Browne, ed., *The Every-Day Life of Abraham Lincoln* (New York: N. D. Thompson, 1886), 663. Miers, ed., *Lincoln Day By Day*, does not confirm this meeting. But Bross, a former editor of the *Chicago Press and Tribune*, had known Lincoln well in Illinois and did have a brother who was killed leading the 29th U.S. Colored Troops, a black regiment from Illinois, at the Battle of the Crater (July 30, 1864) outside Petersburg.

30. Quoted in Browne, ed., *Every-Day Life of Abraham Lincoln*, 667.

31. Neely, "Lincoln Theme since Randall's Call," 18–19. David Donald reaches exactly the opposite conclusion in his well-regarded biography of Lincoln. Donald reads the blind memorandum as a way to demonstrate that Lincoln "did not think the Democrats were disloyal." See Donald, *Lincoln*, 529.

32. Nicolay and Hay, *Abraham Lincoln*, 9:221; Waugh, *Reelecting Lincoln*, 269.

33. Thurlow Weed to William Henry Seward, September 20, 1864, Abraham Lincoln Papers, Library of Congress, Washington.

34. *New York Herald*, August 23, 1864.

35. Burlingame and Ettlinger, eds., *Inside Lincoln's White House*, 248.

36. "Reply to a Serenade," November 10, 1864, in *Collected Works*, 8:100–101.

4. Abraham Lincoln as Moral Leader: The Second Inaugural as America's Sermon to the World / Harry S. Stout

1. James Tackach, *Lincoln's Moral Vision: The Second Inaugural Address* (Jackson: University Press of Mississippi, 2002); and Ronald C. White Jr., *Lincoln's Greatest Speech: The Second Inaugural* (New York: Simon & Schuster, 2002). One important Lincoln study, *On Hallowed Ground: Abraham Lincoln and the Foundations of American History* (New Haven: Yale University Press, 2000), by John Patrick Diggins, does not even mention the Second Inaugural.

2. Frederick Douglass, *Autobiographies* (New York: Library of America, 1994), 801.

3. Mark A. Noll, *America's God from Jonathan Edwards to Abraham Lincoln* (New York: Oxford University Press, 2002), 426; White, *Lincoln's Greatest Speech*, 88; Allen C. Guelzo, *Abraham Lincoln: Redeemer President* (Grand Rapids, MI: Eerdmans, 1999), 414–20; Richard Carwardine, *Lincoln: A Life of Purpose and Power* (New York: Knopf, 2006), 246.

4. See Fred Samkin, "Scripture Notes to Lincoln's Second Inaugural," *Civil War History* 27 (June 1981): 172–73. For the text of the Second Inaugural, see the appendix to this chapter. All quotations from the Second Inaugural in this chapter are from that text, which can also be found in "Second Inaugural Address," March 4, 1865, in Roy P. Basler et al., eds., *The Collected Works of Abraham Lincoln*, 9 vols. (New Brunswick: Rutgers University Press, 1953), 8:332–33 (hereafter *Collected Works*).

5. David H. Donald, *Lincoln* (New York: Simon & Schuster, 1995), 282–84.

6. Garry Wills, *Lincoln at Gettysburg: The Words That Remade America* (New York: Simon & Schuster, 1992), 38.

7. Abraham Lincoln (hereafter AL) to Albert G. Hodges, April 4, 1864, in *Abraham Lincoln: Speeches and Writings, 1859–1865* (New York: Library of America, 1989), 586.

8. Douglass, *Autobiographies*, 789.

9. David W. Blight, *Race and Reunion: The Civil War in American Memory* (Cambridge: Harvard University Press, 2001), 3.

10. Douglass, *Autobiographies*, 789.

11. Harry S. Stout et al., eds., *Sermons and Discourses, 1739–1742* in *The Works of Jonathan Edwards*, vol. 22 (New Haven: Yale University Press, 2003), 406.

12. On Lincoln's religion, see especially Guelzo, *Abraham Lincoln*, 153, 419.

13. AL to Thurlow Weed, March 15, 1865, in *Collected Works*, 8:356.

14. Perry Miller, *The New England Mind: The Seventeenth Century* (Cambridge: Harvard University Press, 1939); and Sacvan Bercovitch, *The American Jeremiad* (Madison: University of Wisconsin Press, 1978).

15. I address this theme extensively in *Upon the Altar of the Nation: A Moral History of the Civil War* (New York: Viking, 2006).

16. Psalms 19:9.

17. See Donald, *Lincoln*, 566.

18. Reprinted in White, *Lincoln's Greatest Speech*, 209.

19. See James M. McPherson, *For Cause and Comrades: Why Men Fought in the Civil War* (New York: Oxford University Press, 1997), 4–5.

20. AL to Albert G. Hodges, April 4, 1864, in *Collected Works*, 7:281.

21. Allen C. Guelzo, *Lincoln's Emancipation Proclamation: The End of Slavery in America* (New York: Simon & Schuster, 2004).

5. Lincoln and Leadership: An Afterword / Allen C. Guelzo

1. Charles S. Moorhead, "Important Statement by the Ex-Governor of Kentucky," *Mississippi Valley Historical Review* 28 (June 1941): 67.

2. David Davis to Leonard Swett, November 26, 1862, in Paul Angle, ed., *Concerning Mr. Lincoln, in Which Abraham Lincoln Is Pictured as He Appeared to Letter Writers of His Time* (Springfield, IL: Abraham Lincoln Association, 1944), 97.

3. Enos Clarke, in Ida M. Tarbell, *The Life of Abraham Lincoln*, 2 vols. (New York: McClure, Phillips, 1904), 2:175.

4. Noah Brooks, "Personal Recollections of Abraham Lincoln," *Harper's New Monthly Magazine* 31 (July 1865): 228.

5. Noah Brooks, "Personal Reminiscences of Lincoln," *Scribner's Monthly* 15 (March 1878): 674.

6. Welles diary entry for July 14, 1863, in John T. Morse, ed., *Diary of Gideon Welles, Secretary of the Navy under Lincoln and Johnson*, 3 vols. (Boston: Houghton Mifflin, 1911), 1:370.

7. Abraham Lincoln (hereafter AL) to Cuthbert Bullitt, July 28, 1862, in Roy P. Basler et al., eds., *Collected Works of Abraham Lincoln*, 9 vols. (New Brunswick: Rutgers University Press, 1953), 5:346 (hereafter *Collected Works*).

8. William H. Herndon, *The Hidden Lincoln: From the Letters and Papers of William H. Herndon* (New York: Blue Ribbon, 1940), 77.

9. Hay diary entry for November 11, 1864, in Michael Burlingame and J. R. T. Ettlinger, eds., *Inside Lincoln's White House: The Complete Civil War Diary of John Hay* (Carbondale: Southern Illinois University Press, 1997), 249.

10. William H, Herndon to C. O. Poole, January 5, 1886, in Herndon, *The Hidden Lincoln*, 120.

11. George Borrett, *Out West: Letters from Canada and the United States* (London: Groombridge & Sons, 1866), 252–53.

12. Leonard Swett to William H. Herndon, January 17, 1866, in Rodney O. Davis and Douglas L. Wilson, eds., *Herndon's Informants: Letters, Interviews, and Statements about Abraham Lincoln* (Urbana: University of Illinois Press, 1998), 167.

13. Hay diary entry for September 24, 1862, in Burlingame and Ettlinger, eds., *Inside Lincoln's White House*, 41.

14. AL, "Fragment: Notes for a Law Lecture," July 1, 1850, in Roy P. Basler, ed., *The Collected Works of Abraham Lincoln: Supplement, 1832–1865* (Westport, CT: Greenwood, 1974), 19; and AL to John M. Brockman, September 25, 1860, in *Collected Works*, 4:121.

15. David Davis interview with William H. Herndon, September 20, 1866, in Davis and Wilson, eds., *Herndon's Informants*, 349.

16. "Editorial Method," in Daniel W. Stowell et al., eds., *The Papers of Abraham Lincoln: Legal Documents and Cases*, 4 vols. (Charlottesville: University of Virginia Press, 2008), 1:xix.

17. Isaac Newton Arnold, *The Life of Abraham Lincoln* (Chicago: Jansen, McClurg, 1885), 84.

18. George Boutwell, in Allen Thorndike Rice, ed., *Reminiscences of Abraham Lincoln by Distinguished Men of His Time* (New York: North American Publishing, 1886), 132.

19. John Hay to John G. Nicolay, August 7 and September 11, 1863, in Michael Burlingame, ed., *At Lincoln's Side: John Hay's Civil War Correspondence and Selected Writings* (Carbondale: Southern Illinois University Press, 2000), 54.

20. AL to Joshua F. Speed, February 13, 1842, in *Collected Works*, 1:269-70.

21. Robert Lincoln to Isaac Markens, March 5, 1918, in Paul M. Angle, ed., *A Portrait of Abraham Lincoln in Letters by His Oldest Son* (Chicago: Chicago Historical Society, 1968), 56.

22. Leonard Swett to William Herndon, January 17, 1866, in Davis and Wilson, eds., *Herndon's Informants*, 167.

23. John Hay to William Herndon, September 5, 1866, in Burlingame, ed., *At Lincoln's Side*, 110.

24. Vachel Lindsay, "Abraham Lincoln Walks at Midnight," *The Independent* 79 (September 21, 1914): 408.

Bibliographical Essay

The literature on Abraham Lincoln and leadership is vast and growing. Indeed, anticipating the bicentennial year of his birth, scholars from several fields offered major new assessments of Lincoln as a political, military, intellectual, religious, and even "literary" leader. The scholarship promises to continue unabated, at least for a time. As new Lincoln materials come to light—for example, in the recent mining of Lincoln's legal papers—new perspectives on and new insights into Lincoln's character and interests will emerge and refinements and revisions of older interpretations will occur. Then, too, the centrality of Lincoln to Americans' sense of themselves and their basic principles continues to spur interest in understanding the man and his time. And, in the end, Lincoln still fascinates. The many masks and the very private nature of perhaps America's most public face constantly invite inquiry.

This bibliographical essay focuses on books relating to aspects of Lincoln as a public person in politics and in governing. It principally draws on more recent treatments in pointing to the lines of inquiry about Lincoln and his leadership, though it also suggests important Lincoln-related works that reveal his sources and patterns of thought, and his relations with political, military, and social leaders. As such, it hardly captures the enormous Lincoln literature, so much of which is in scholarly and popular journals. Following the reference trail to such works by using the following books should chart the way to the important studies in journal and magazine form.

The best way to enter the large and sometimes tangled terrain of Lincoln scholarship is through the recent assessments by some of the most distinguished students of the man and his age. Very useful in that regard are the essays in Eric Foner, ed., *Our Lincoln: New Perspectives on Lincoln and His World* (New York: Norton, 2008), which survey Lincoln in such categories as the president, the emancipator, the man, and politics and memory. Also instructive is John Y. Simon, Harold Holzer, and Dawn Vogel, eds., *Lincoln Revisited: New Insights from the Lincoln Forum* (New York: Fordham University Press, 2007), which covers a wide range of topics, from politics, to religion, to race, to relations with generals, to civil liberties, to name several subjects in the collection. The essays in part 2, "The Leader and the Legacy: Politics, Patriotism, and the Civil War," in Susan-Mary Grant and Peter J. Parish, eds., *Legacy of Disunion: The Enduring Significance of the American Civil War* (Baton Rouge: Louisiana State University Press, 2003), also repay reading. So, too, do the essays and commentary in Gabor S. Boritt, ed., *The Historian's Lincoln: Pseudohistory, Psychohistory, and History* (Urbana: University of Illinois Press, 1988). For an intelligent collection of "classic" essays on Lincoln, see Sean Wilentz, ed., *The Best American History Essays on Lincoln* (New York: Palgrave Macmillan, 2009). Orville Vernon Burton, *The Age of Lincoln* (New York: Hill & Wang, 2007), is a major interpretation of the nineteenth-century United States that places Lincoln at the vital center of American identity.

Getting to know Lincoln requires reading his own words. Small collections of Lincoln letters and other documents exist in repositories across the country, as do individual Lincoln items. A full inventory of such works remains in the making. Happily, Daniel W. Stowell and the Lincoln Papers project is gathering together all known Lincoln papers, including many newly discovered legal documents, to provide a "comprehensive" archive. The fullest single collection of Lincoln's papers, essential to any understanding of the dynamics of his leadership, is the Robert Todd Lincoln Collection in the Library of Congress, which consists largely of incoming correspondence. The most complete published collection of Lincoln's own writings (letters, speeches, memos) is Roy P. Basler et al., eds., *The Collected Works of Abraham Lincoln*, 9 vols. (New Brunswick: Rutgers University Press, 1953–55); Roy P. Basler, ed., *The Collected Works of Abraham Lincoln: Supplement, 1832–1865* (Westport, CT: Greenwood, 1974); and Roy P. Basler and Christian O. Basler, eds., *The Collected Works of Abraham Lincoln: Second Supplement, 1848–1865* (New Brunswick: Rutgers University Press, 1990). Also, Lincoln's legal papers are now available: see Martha L. Benner and Cullom Davis, eds., *The Law Practice of Abraham Lincoln: Complete Documentary Edition*, 3 DVDs (Urbana: University of Illinois Press, 2000); and Daniel W. Stowell, ed., *Papers of Abraham Lincoln: Legal Documents and Cases*, 4 vols. (Charlottesville: University of Virginia Press, 2007). The most useful anthologies of Lincoln's writings are Don E. Fehrenbacher, ed., *Abraham Lincoln: Speeches and Writings*, 2 vols. (New York: Library of America, 1989); Mario Cuomo and Harold Holzer, eds., *Lincoln on Democracy: His Own Words, with Essays by America's Foremost Civil War Historians* (New York: HarperCollins, 1990); Andrew Delbanco, ed., *The Portable Abraham Lincoln* (New York: Viking Penguin, 1992); William Gienapp, ed., *This Fiery Trial: The Speeches and Writings of Abraham Lincoln* (New York: Oxford University Press, 2002); and Michael P. Johnson, *Abraham Lincoln, Slavery, and the Civil War: Selected Writings and Speeches* (Boston: Bedford/St. Martin's, 2001). For a reliable collection of Lincoln quotations, as related by the many people who recalled and recorded conversations with Lincoln, see Don E. Fehrenbacher and Virginia Fehrenbacher, eds., *Recollected Words of Abraham Lincoln* (Stanford: Stanford University Press, 1996).

The biographical literature is massive, even daunting. Among recent works, the best place to begin is James M. McPherson, *Abraham Lincoln* (New York: Oxford University Press, 2009), which succinctly presents the Pulitzer Prize–winning historian's measured arguments from his many other works. Also perceptive in short compass are Allen C. Guelzo, *Lincoln: A Very Short Introduction* (New York: Oxford University Press, 2009); and Thomas Keneally, *Abraham Lincoln* (New York: Viking, 2003). Important, more substantial biographies include Michael Burlingame, *Abraham Lincoln: A Life*, 2 vols. (Baltimore: Johns Hopkins University Press, 2009), which covers almost every aspect of Lincoln's life in encyclopedic detail and with perceptive insight; Richard Carwardine, *Lincoln: A Life of Purpose and Power* (New York: Knopf, 2006), which offers a British perspective and emphasizes Lincoln's moral power; David Herbert Donald, *Lincoln* (New York: Simon & Schuster, 1995), which stands as the fullest single-volume treatment; William E. Gienapp, *Abraham Lincoln and Civil War America: A Biography* (New York: Oxford University Press, 2002), which provides a perceptive analysis of Lincoln's public life; Allen C.

Guelzo, *Abraham Lincoln as a Man of Ideas* (Carbondale: Southern Illinois University Press, 2009), which probes Lincoln's thought and his thinking processes; Mark E. Neely Jr., *The Last Best Hope of Earth: Abraham Lincoln and the Promise of America* (Cambridge: Harvard University Press, 1993), which richly illustrates Lincoln's thought and policies; Ronald C. White, *A. Lincoln: A Biography* (New York: Random House, 2009), which especially provides insights into Lincoln's sources and uses of thought and belief; Thomas Schneider, *Lincoln's Defense of Politics: The Public Man and His Opponents in the Crisis over Slavery* (Columbia: University of Missouri Press, 2006), which sets Lincoln's political thoughts in context; and William Lee Miller, *President Lincoln: The Duty of a Statesman* (New York: Knopf, 2008), which emphasizes moral questions. Among older works, Benjamin P. Thomas, *Abraham Lincoln: A Biography* (New York: Knopf, 1952), remains a useful one-volume study. David Donald, *Lincoln Reconsidered: Essays on the Civil War Era* (New York: Knopf, 1956), still provokes thought with arguments about Lincoln's identity and interests that have stirred work for half a century. Richard N. Current, *The Lincoln Nobody Knows* (New York: Hill & Wang, 1958), also has proved remarkably durable. Gabor S. Boritt, ed., *The Lincoln Enigma: The Changing Faces of an American Icon* (New York: Oxford University Press, 2001), provides many angles from which to see Lincoln the man and his leadership. Lincoln's pre-presidential years are most fully and perceptively developed in Don E. Fehrenbacher, *Prelude to Greatness: Lincoln in the 1850s* (Stanford: Stanford University Press, 1962); Robert W. Johannsen, *Lincoln, the South, and Slavery* (Baton Rouge: Louisiana State University Press, 1991); John C. Waugh, *One Man Great Enough: Abraham Lincoln's Road to Civil War* (New York: Harcourt, 2007); Roy Morris Jr., *The Long Pursuit: Abraham Lincoln's Thirty-Year Struggle with Stephen Douglas for the Heart and Soul of America* (Washington, DC: Smithsonian Books, 2008); William C. Harris, *Lincoln's Rise to the Presidency* (Lawrence: University Press of Kansas, 2007), which points to his respect for the Constitution and Whig ideals as touchstones; Kenneth J. Winkle, *The Young Eagle: The Rise of Abraham Lincoln* (Dallas: Taylor, 2001), which places the young Lincoln in the social contexts of migration; Roger Billings and Frank J. Williams, eds., *A. Lincoln, Esq.: The Legal Career of America's Greatest President* (Lexington: University Press of Kentucky, 2010), an anthology on Lincoln's law practices and skills; Mark Steiner, *An Honest Calling: The Law Practice of Abraham Lincoln* (DeKalb: Northern Illinois University Press, 2009); and Harry V. Jaffa, *A New Birth of Freedom: Abraham Lincoln and the Coming of the Civil War* (Lanham, MD: Rowman & Littlefield, 2000), which follows his seminal *A Crisis of the House Divided: An Interpretation of the Issues in the Lincoln-Douglas Debates* (New York: Doubleday, 1959), showing how and why Lincoln, more than anyone else, understood the imperatives of stopping slavery's advance and keeping the Union intact. For a detailed catalog of Lincoln's early years, see Richard Lawrence Miller, *Lincoln and His World: The Early Years, Birth to Illinois Legislature* (Mechanicsburg, PA: Stackpole, 2006); and Miller, *Lincoln and His World: Prairie Politician, 1834–1842* (Mechanicsburg, PA: Stackpole, 2008). In a large literature on the Lincoln-Douglas debates, Allen C. Guelzo, *Lincoln and Douglas: The Debates That Defined America* (New York: Simon & Schuster, 2008), supersedes previous work. Richard W. Etulain, *Lincoln Looks West: From the Mississippi to the Pacific* (Carbondale: Southern Illinois University Press, 2010), provides a much-needed assessment of Lincoln's western vision and policies from his Whiggish youth through his presidency. Lincoln's Indian policies remain understudied, but David A. Nichols, *Lincoln and the Indians: Civil War Policy and Politics* (Columbia: University of Missouri Press, 1978), is the place to start.

Lincoln's marriage to Mary Todd Lincoln has occasioned much comment, though not so much critical assessment as it relates to Lincoln's interests in politics, public policy, and the presidency. Especially instructive about the marriage and Lincoln's family life as it informed and affected his leadership are Jean H. Baker, *Mary Todd Lincoln: A Biography* (New York: Norton, 1987); David Herbert Donald, *Lincoln at Home: Two Glimpses of Abraham Lincoln's Family Life* (New York: Simon & Schuster, 1999); Jerrold M. Packard, *The Lincolns in the White House: Four Years That Shattered a Family* (New York: St. Martin's Griffin, 2005); Catherine Clinton, *Mrs. Lincoln: A Life* (New York: HarperCollins, 2009); Stephen Berry, *House of Abraham: Lincoln and the Todds, a Family Divided by War* (Boston: Houghton Mifflin, 2007); and despite some errors in fact and misdirection, Daniel Mark Epstein, *The Lincolns: Portrait of a Marriage* (New York; Ballantine, 2008). Also useful in considering Mary Todd Lincoln's role in her husband's political maturation and national ambitions is W. A. Evans, *Mrs. Abraham Lincoln: A Study of Her Personality and Her Influence on Lincoln* (Carbondale: Southern Illinois University Press, 2010). In a class by itself is Michael Burlingame, *The Inner World of Abraham Lincoln* (Urbana: University of Illinois Press, 1994), which offers a probing psychobiography of Lincoln that relates his difficult family life, troubled relations with women, and private mental torments to his ideas and his public persona.

On Lincoln's presidency, Phillip Shaw Paludan, *The Presidency of Abraham Lincoln* (Lawrence: University Press of Kansas, 1994), is indispensable. Also significant are William Lee Miller, *President Lincoln: The Duty of a Statesman* (New York: Knopf, 2008); and Charles M. Hubbard, ed., *Lincoln Reshapes the Presidency, 1861* (Macon: Mercer University Press, 2003). Earlier work that still commands attention includes the four-volume study by James G. Randall, *Lincoln the President*, 2 vols. (New York: Dodd, Mead, 1945); Randall, *Lincoln the President: Midstream* (New York: Dodd, Mead, 1953); and Randall, with Richard N. Current, *Lincoln the President: The Last Full Measure* (New York: Dodd, Mead, 1955). On Lincoln as president-elect and his decision making in the fateful days before his inauguration and shortly thereafter, see especially Harold Holzer, *Lincoln President-Elect: Abraham Lincoln and the Great Secession Winter, 1860–1861* (New York: Simon & Schuster, 2008); and Russell McClintock, *Lincoln and the Decision for War: The Northern Response to Secession* (Chapel Hill: University of North Carolina Press, 2008). Also significant are Maury Klein, *Days of Defiance: Sumter, Secession, and the Coming of the Civil War* (New York: Knopf, 1997); David M. Potter, *Lincoln and His Party in the Secession Crisis* (New Haven: Yale University Press, 1942); Kenneth M. Stampp, *And the War Came: The North and the Secession Crisis* (Baton Rouge: Louisiana State University Press, 1950); Shearer Davis Bowman, *At the Precipice: Americans North and South during the Secession Crisis* (Chapel Hill: University of North Carolina Press, 2010); and Emory M. Thomas, *The Dogs of War, 1861* (New York: Oxford University Press, 2011). For a very "contrarian" view of Lincoln's decisions leading to war, see William Marvel, *Mr. Lincoln Goes to War* (Boston: Houghton Mifflin, 2006), which is a far step away from most scholarly assessments of Lincoln's leadership. On Lincoln's last days in office, see William C. Harris, *Lincoln's Last Months* (Cambridge: Harvard University Press, 2004). On the public response to his death, see Thomas Reed Turner, *"Beware the People Weeping": Public Opinion and the Assassination of Abraham Lincoln* (Baton Rouge: Louisiana State University Press, 1982); Carolyn L. Harrell, *When the Bells Tolled for Lincoln: Southern Reaction to the Assassination* (Macon: Mercer University Press, 1997); and Harold Holzer, Craig L. Symonds, and Frank J. Williams, eds., *The Lincoln Assassination: Crime and Punishment, Myth and Memory* (New York: Fordham University Press, 2010).

On the politics of Lincoln's day and his political leadership, see Doris Kearns Goodwin, *Team of Rivals: The Political Genius of Abraham Lincoln* (New York: Simon & Schuster, 2005); Michael S. Green, *Freedom, Union, and Power: Lincoln and His Party during the Civil War* (New York: Fordham University Press, 2004); Gary Ecelbarger, *The Great Comeback: How Abraham Lincoln Beat the Odds to Win the 1860 Republican Nomination* (New York: St. Martin's, 2008); Douglas R. Egerton, *Year of Meteors: Stephen Douglas, Abraham Lincoln, and the Election That Brought on the Civil War* (New York: Bloomsbury, 2010); William Marvel, *Lincoln's Darkest Year: The War in 1862* (New York: Houghton Mifflin, 2008); William Marvel, *The Great Task Remaining: The Third Year of Lincoln's War* (Boston: Houghton Mifflin, 2010); Charles Bracelen Flood, *1864: Lincoln at the Gates of History* (New York: Simon & Schuster, 2009); David E. Long, *The Jewel of Liberty: Abraham Lincoln's Re-election and the End of Slavery* (Mechanicsburg, PA: Stackpole, 1994); the Civil War–era essays in John L. Thomas, ed., *Abraham Lincoln and the American Political Tradition* (Amherst: University of Massachusetts Press, 1986); James A. Rawley, ed., *Lincoln and Civil War Politics* (New York: Holt, Rinehart & Winston, 1969); John C. Waugh, *Reelecting Lincoln: The Battle for the 1864 Presidency* (New York: Crown, 1997); and William F. Zornow, *Lincoln and the Party Divided* (Norman: University of Oklahoma Press, 1964). Still instructive are William B. Hesseltine, *Lincoln and the War Governors* (New York: Knopf, 1955); Burton J. Hendrick, *Lincoln's War Cabinet* (Boston: Little, Brown, 1946); and T. Harry Williams, *Lincoln and the Radicals* (Madison: University of Wisconsin Press, 1941), which should be balanced with Hans L. Trefousse, *The Radical Republicans: Lincoln's Vanguard for Racial Justice* (New York: Knopf, 1969). A good short essay on Lincoln's political style and interest is Richard Norton Smith, *Abraham Lincoln and the Triumph of Politics* (Gettysburg, PA: Gettysburg College, 2007). Also revealing about Lincoln's political character is David Herbert Donald, *"We Are Lincoln Men": Abraham Lincoln and His Friends* (New York: Simon & Schuster, 2003). Matthew Pinsker, *Lincoln's Sanctuary: Abraham Lincoln and the Soldiers' Home* (New York: Oxford University Press, 2003), says much about Lincoln's work habits and personal life as they informed his political relationships. Daniel Mark Epstein, *Lincoln's Men: The President and His Private Secretaries* (New York: Smithsonian Books, 2009), gives an inside-the-White-House perspective on Lincoln at work. Hans L. Trefousse, *"First among Equals": Abraham Lincoln's Reputation during His Administration* (New York: Fordham University Press, 2005), corrects many misconceptions regarding Lincoln's standing. A forceful defense of Lincoln's principles and Lincoln's relations with the press are most recently given in Harry J. Maihafer, *War*

of Words: Abraham Lincoln and the Civil War Press (Washington, DC: Brassey's, 2001).
For overviews and analyses of the Republicans in Lincoln's day, see Herman Belz, *A New
Birth of Freedom: The Republican Party and Freedmen's Rights, 1861–1866* (Westport, CT:
Greenwood, 1976); Robert F. Engs and Randall M. Miller, eds., *The Birth of the Grand Old
Party: The Republicans' First Generation* (Philadelphia: University of Pennsylvania Press,
2002); Mark E. Neely Jr., *The Union Divided: Party Conflict in the Civil War North* (Cam-
bridge: Harvard University Press, 2002); and Adam I. P. Smith, *No Party Now: Politics in
the Civil War North* (New York: Oxford University Press, 2006). Eric Foner, *Free Soil, Free
Labor, Free Men: The Ideology of the Republican Party before the Civil War* (New York: Oxford University Press, 1970), remains the starting point for understanding the arguments,
interests, and issues shaping the Republican Party. But see also William E. Gienapp, *The
Origins of the Republican Party, 1852–1856* (New York: Oxford University Press, 1987), for
the party formation that drew Lincoln to the Republicans.

On Lincoln as commander in chief, James McPherson, *Tried by War: Abraham Lincoln
as Commander in Chief* (New York: Penguin, 2008), stands above all other treatments.
Also significant are Geoffrey Perret, *Lincoln's War: The Untold Story of America's Greatest
President as Commander in Chief* (New York: Random House, 2004); Gabor S. Boritt,
ed., *Lincoln the War President: The Gettysburg Lectures* (New York: Oxford University
Press, 1992); Gabor S. Boritt, ed., *Lincoln's Generals* (New York: Oxford University Press,
1994); David Work, *Lincoln's Political Generals* (Urbana: University of Illinois Press, 2009);
John C. Waugh, *Lincoln and McClellan: The Troubled Partnership between a President and
His General* (New York: Palgrave Macmillan, 2010); Chester G. Hearn, *Lincoln, the Cabi-
net, and the Generals* (Baton Rouge: Louisiana State University Press, 2010); and James M.
McPherson, *Abraham Lincoln and the Second American Revolution* (New York: Oxford
University Press, 1991). T. Harry Williams, *Lincoln and His Generals* (New York: Knopf,
1952), remains important reading, though other historians have challenged his arguments
as to Lincoln's astute strategic abilities. On strategic considerations, Donald Stoker, *The
Grand Design: Strategy and the U.S. Civil War* (New York: Oxford University Press, 2010),
provides a good overview. On Lincoln's relationships with Congress over war policy, see
Bruce Tap, *Over Lincoln's Shoulder: The Committee on the Conduct of the War* (Lawrence:
University Press of Kansas, 1998). William C. Davis, *Lincoln's Men: How President Lincoln
Became Father to an Army and a Nation* (New York: Free Press, 1999), reveals Lincoln's
special relationship with Union soldiers. Craig L. Symonds, *Lincoln and His Admirals*
(New York: Oxford University Press, 2008), astutely examines Lincoln as admiral in chief.
Useful in placing Lincoln's role in foreign policy in context—a subject neglected in this
volume—is Howard Jones, *Blue and Gray Diplomacy: A History of Union and Confederate
Foreign Relations* (Chapel Hill: University of North Carolina Press, 2010).

On constitutional issues arising during Lincoln's presidency, see Mark E. Neely Jr.,
Lincoln and the Triumph of the Nation: Constitutional Conflict in the American Civil War
(Chapel Hill: University of North Carolina Press, 2011); Herman Belz, *Abraham Lincoln,
Constitutionalism, and Equal Rights in the Civil War Era* (New York: Fordham University
Press, 1998); Daniel Farber, *Lincoln's Constitution* (Chicago: University of Chicago Press,
2003); Brian McGinty, *Lincoln and the Court* (Cambridge: Harvard University Press,

2008); James F. Simon, *Lincoln and Chief Justice Taney: Slavery, Secession, and the President's War Powers* (New York: Simon & Schuster, 2006); and George P. Fletcher, *Our Secret Constitution: How Lincoln Redefined American Democracy* (New York: Oxford University Press, 2001). More generally, Harold M. Hyman and William M. Wiecek, *Equal Justice under the Law: Constitutional Development, 1835–1875* (New York: Harper & Row, 1982), remains unimpeachable; Phillip Shaw Paludan, *A Covenant with Death: The Constitution, Law, and Equality in the Civil War Era* (Urbana: University of Illinois Press, 1975), remains reliable; and James G. Randall, *Constitutional Problems under Lincoln* (Urbana: University of Illinois Press, 1951), remains relevant. On Lincoln and civil liberties, Mark E. Neely Jr., *The Fate of Liberty: Abraham Lincoln and Civil Liberties* (New York: Oxford University Press, 1991), is essential.

On Lincoln, slavery, race, and politics, see especially Eric Foner, *The Fiery Trial: Abraham Lincoln and American Slavery* (New York: Norton, 2010), which synthesizes much recent literature and offers a balanced consideration of Lincoln's commitment to antislavery principles and his evolving ideas about race. Also instructive, though hardly in agreement, are James Oakes, *The Radical and the Republican: Frederick Douglass, Abraham Lincoln, and the Triumph of Antislavery Politics* (New York: Norton, 2007); Paul D. Escott, *"What Shall We Do with the Negro?": Lincoln, White Racism, and Civil War America* (Charlottesville: University of Virginia Press, 2009); George Fredrickson, *Big Enough to Be Inconsistent: Abraham Lincoln Confronts Slavery and Race* (Cambridge: Harvard University Press, 2008); Brian Dirck, ed., *Lincoln Emancipated: The President and the Politics of Race* (DeKalb: Northern Illinois University Press, 2007); Benjamin Quarles, *Lincoln and the Negro* (New York: Oxford University Press, 1962); Paul Kendrick and Stephen Kendrick, *Douglass and Lincoln: How a Revolutionary Black Leader and a Reluctant Liberator Struggled to End Slavery and Save the Union* (New York: Walker, 2008); John Stauffer, *Giants: The Parallel Lives of Frederick Douglass and Abraham Lincoln* (New York: Twelve, 2009); Richard Striner, *Father Abraham: Lincoln's Relentless Struggle to End Slavery* (New York: Oxford University Press, 2006); Harold Holzer and Sara Vaughn Gabbard, eds., *Lincoln and Freedom: Slavery, Emancipation, and the Thirteenth Amendment* (Carbondale: Southern Illinois University Press, 2007); Howard Jones, *Abraham Lincoln and the New Birth of Freedom: The Union and Slavery in the Diplomacy of the Civil War* (Lincoln: University of Nebraska Press, 1999); and Michael Vorenberg, *Final Freedom: The Civil War, the Abolition of Slavery, and the Thirteenth Amendment* (New York: Cambridge University Press, 2001). On Lincoln and Reconstruction, the best starting point is Eric Foner, *Reconstruction: America's Unfinished Business, 1863–1877* (New York: Harper & Row, 1988), for the overall assessment of presidential interest and policy. It should be read along with William C. Harris, *With Charity for All: Lincoln and the Restoration of the Union* (Lexington: University Press of Kentucky, 1997); Herman Belz, *Reconstructing the Union: Theory and Policy during the Civil War* (Ithaca: Cornell University Press, 1969); Michael Les Benedict, *A Compromise of Principle: Congressional Republicans and Reconstruction* (New York: Norton, 1974); Peyton McCrary, *Abraham Lincoln and Reconstruction: The Louisiana Experiment* (Princeton: Princeton University Press, 1978); and Harold M. Hyman, *Lincoln's Reconstruction: Neither Failure of Vision nor Vision of Failure* (Fort Wayne, IN: Louis A.

Warren Lincoln Library and Museum, 1980), for the particulars. The section on Lincoln in Brooks D. Simpson, *The Reconstruction Presidents* (Lawrence: University Press of Kansas, 1998), also repays reading. See also Richard H. Abbott, *The Republican Party and the South: The First Southern Strategy, 1855–1877* (Chapel Hill: University of North Carolina Press, 1986). Despite some errors in fact in the editor's interpretations, Henry Louis Gates Jr., ed., *Lincoln on Race and Slavery* (Princeton: Princeton University Press, 2009), is a valuable collection of Lincoln letters and other documents, with Gates's still instructive commentary.

On the Emancipation Proclamation, see especially Allen C. Guelzo, *Lincoln's Emancipation Proclamation: The End of Slavery in America* (New York: Simon & Schuster, 2004); John Hope Franklin, *The Emancipation Proclamation* (Garden City, NY: Doubleday, 1963); Burrus M. Carnahan, *Act of Justice: Lincoln's Emancipation Proclamation and the Law of War* (Lexington: University Press of Kentucky, 2007); Harold Holzer, Edna Greene Medford, and Frank J. Williams, eds., *The Emancipation Proclamation: Three Views* (Baton Rouge: Louisiana State University Press, 2006); William A. Blair and Karen Fisher Younger, eds., *Lincoln's Proclamation: Emancipation Reconsidered* (Chapel Hill: University of North Carolina Press, 2009); and Michael Vorenberg, ed., *The Emancipation Proclamation: A Brief History with Documents* (Boston: Bedford/St. Martin's, 2010). Still valuable on Lincoln's role in advancing black freedom is LaWanda Cox, *Lincoln and Black Freedom: A Study in Presidential Leadership* (Columbia: University of South Carolina Press, 1981).

The construction, uses, and effects of Lincoln's speeches and other writings have generated a contentious literature. Important to understanding the subject are Gary Wills, *Lincoln at Gettysburg: The Words That Remade America* (New York: Simon & Schuster, 1992), which has defined the issues for the past generation, if it also has, by some reckonings, also misdirected the emphasis; Ronald C. White Jr., *The Eloquent President: A Portrait of Lincoln through His Words* (New York: Random House, 2005); John Channing Briggs, *Lincoln's Speeches Reconsidered* (Baltimore: Johns Hopkins University Press, 2005); and Douglas Wilson, *Lincoln's Sword: The Presidency and the Power of Words* (New York: Knopf, 2006). Gabor S. Boritt, *The Gettysburg Gospel: The Lincoln Speech That Nobody Knows* (New York: Simon & Schuster, 2006), reconstructs the time, place, and telling of the Address. Lincoln's earlier speeches have received close attention in Lewis E. Lehrman, *Lincoln at Peoria: The Turning Point* (Mechanicsburg, PA: Stackpole, 2008); and Harold Holzer, *Lincoln at Cooper Union: The Speech That Made Abraham Lincoln President* (New York: Simon & Schuster, 2004). Lewis Fred Kaplan, *Lincoln: The Biography of a Writer* (New York: HarperCollins, 2008), makes the case that Lincoln led because of his literary genius. Robert Bray, *Reading with Lincoln* (Carbondale: Southern Illinois University Press, 2010), connects Lincoln's lifetime of reading to his intellectual and political development.

On the theological issues and moral sensibilities raised by the war and Lincoln's wrestling with them, see Mark A. Noll, *The Civil War as a Theological Crisis* (Chapel Hill: University of North Carolina Press, 2006); William Lee Miller, *Lincoln's Virtues: An Ethical Biography* (New York: Knopf, 2002), which emphasizes the moral choices Lincoln confronted in politics and his own life; and for a more critical perspective, Harry S. Stout, *Upon the Altar of the Nation: A Moral History of the Civil War* (New York: Viking, 2006).

On Lincoln's religion and its place in his public life, see especially Allen C. Guelzo, *Abraham Lincoln: Redeemer President* (Grand Rapids, MI: Eerdmans, 1999), a major work that has reoriented views on the subject; and Ronald C. White Jr., *Lincoln's Greatest Speech: The Second Inaugural* (New York: Simon & Schuster, 2002). See also James Tackach, *Lincoln's Moral Vision: The Second Inaugural Address* (Jackson: University Press of Mississippi, 2002); Joseph R. Fornieri, *Abraham Lincoln's Political Faith* (DeKalb: Northern Illinois University Press, 2003), which is more political theory than history; Lucas E. Morel, *Lincoln's Sacred Effort: Defining Religion's Role in American Self-Government* (Lanham, MD: Lexington, 2000); William J. Wolf, *The Almost Chosen People: A Study of the Religion of Abraham Lincoln* (Garden City, NY: Doubleday, 1959); Wayne C. Temple, *Abraham Lincoln: From Skeptic to Prophet* (Mahomet, IL: Mayhaven, 1995); Stewart Winger, *Lincoln, Religion, and Romantic Cultural Politics* (DeKalb: Northern Illinois University Press, 2003); and with some reservations, Allen Jayne, *Lincoln and the American Manifesto* (Amherst, NY: Prometheus, 2007).

The importance of Lincoln in illustration and photography has generated a significant scholarship. For excellent examples and informed context, see Harold Holzer, Gabor S. Boritt, and Mark E. Neely Jr., *The Lincoln Image: Abraham Lincoln and the Popular Print* (New York: Scribner, 1984); and Stefan Lorant, *Lincoln: A Picture Story of His Life* (rev. and enlarged ed., New York: Norton, 1969). Rufus Rockwell Wilson, *Lincoln in Caricature: A Historical Collection* (New York: Horizon, 1953), has many examples of Lincoln caricatures drawn from American and English newspapers and magazines; so, too, does Gary L. Bunker, *From Rail-Splitter to Icon: Lincoln's Image in Illustrated Periodicals, 1860–1865* (Kent: Kent State University Press, 2001). Lloyd Ostendorf, *Lincoln's Photographs: A Complete Album* (Dayton, OH: Rockywood Press, 1998), is a very full portfolio. Philip B. Kunhardt III, Peter W. Kunhardt, and Peter W. Kunhardt Jr., *Lincoln, Life-Size* (New York: Knopf, 2009), presents Lincoln biographically through his photographic portraits. A good short treatment of the Lincoln image is Harold Holzer, *Standing Tall: The Heroic Image of Abraham Lincoln* (Gettysburg, PA: Gettysburg College, 2004).

In addition to the biographies and studies noted above, among reference works, Mark E. Neely Jr., *The Abraham Lincoln Encyclopedia* (New York: McGraw-Hill, 1982), remains most valuable for details and directions in examining Lincoln's life and work. Matthew Pinsker, *Abraham Lincoln* (New York: Times Books, 2002), provides much useful information and many relevant documents. Gerald J. Prokopowicz, *Did Lincoln Own Slaves?, and Other Frequently Asked Questions about Abraham Lincoln* (New York: Vintage, 2008), debunks many myths, corrects many errors, and offers many insights regarding Lincoln's life and others' claims about him. Also revealing and entertaining is Edward Steer, *Lincoln Legends: Myths, Hoaxes, and Confabulations Associated with Our Greatest President* (Lexington: University Press of Kentucky, 2009). Stephen A. Wynalda, *366 Days in Abraham Lincoln's Presidency: The Private, Political, and Military Decisions of America's Greatest President* (New York: Skyhorse, 2010), offers a compendium of Lincoln thought and action arranged chronologically.

On Lincoln's place in the American consciousness, and even conscience, and the changing images of Lincoln and the uses people have made of his memory, Merrill D.

Peterson, *Lincoln in American Memory* (New York: Oxford University Press, 1994), remains essential. Also insightful are Barry Schwartz, *Abraham Lincoln and the Forge of National Memory* (Chicago: University of Chicago Press, 2000); and Schwartz, *Abraham Lincoln in the Post-Heroic Era: History and Memory in Late Twentieth-Century America* (Chicago: University of Chicago Press, 2008). John P. Diggins, *On Hallowed Ground: Abraham Lincoln and the Foundations of American History* (New Haven: Yale University Press, 2000), argues that Lincoln's morality and political faith in the founding principles of the republic shaped American history and continued to provide the cement for American values. Thomas L. Krannawitter, *Vindicating Lincoln: Defending the Politics of Our Greatest President* (Lanham, MD: Rowman & Littlefield, 2008), gives a vigorous rebuttal to recent depictions of Lincoln as a tyrant, a racist, and a betrayer of the nation's trust; and Robert P. Watson, William D. Pederson, and Frank J. Williams, eds., *Lincoln's Enduring Legacy: Perspective from Great Thinkers, Great Leaders, and the American Experiment* (Lanham, MD: Lexington, 2011), offers essays on Lincoln as seen by great men and women over time. For a delightful and insightful search for the Lincoln of myth and memory today, see James A. Percoco, *Summers with Lincoln: Looking for the Monuments* (New York: Fordham University Press, 2008).

Contributors

Allen C. Guelzo is the Henry R. Luce Professor of the Civil War Era and Director of Civil War Studies at Gettysburg College. He is the author of numerous books treating subjects from Jonathan Edwards, to evangelical Christianity, to Lincoln and the Civil War era. Among his recent books are *Abraham Lincoln: Redeemer President* (Eerdmans, 1999), which won the Lincoln Prize for 2000; *Lincoln's Emancipation Proclamation: The End of Slavery in America* (Simon & Schuster, 2004), which won the Lincoln Prize for 2005; *Lincoln and Douglas: The Debates That Defined America* (Simon & Schuster, 2008); *Abraham Lincoln as a Man of Ideas* (Southern Illinois University Press, 2009); and *Lincoln: A Very Short Introduction* (Oxford University Press, 2009).

Randall M. Miller is the William Dirk Warren '05 Sesquicentennial Chair and Professor of History at Saint Joseph's University. He is author or editor of numerous books. Among his books related to the Civil War are, as coeditor, *Religion and the American Civil War* (Oxford University Press, 1998), and *The Birth of the Grand Old Party: The Republicans' First Generation* (University of Pennsylvania Press, 2002). His most recent book, co-authored with Paul Cimbala, is *The Northern Home Front in the Civil War* (Praeger, 2012).

Matthew Pinsker holds the Brian Pohanka Chair for Civil War History at Dickinson College. Among his many interests, he writes on political issues, personalities, and history. In Lincoln studies, he is best known for his highly acclaimed *Lincoln's Sanctuary: Abraham Lincoln and the Soldiers' Home* (Oxford University Press, 2003). He also wrote *Abraham Lincoln* (CQ Press, 2002) for the "American Presidents Reference Series."

Harry S. Stout is the Jonathan Edwards Chair of American Religious History at Yale University. He is the author of several highly regarded books in American religious history. His interests in the Civil War have led to two important books, *Upon the Altar of the Nation: A Moral History of the Civil War* (Viking, 2006), and, as coeditor, *Religion and the American Civil War* (Oxford University Press, 1998).

Gregory J. W. Urwin is Professor of History at Temple University, Vice-President of the Society for Military History, and the General Editor of the "Campaigns and Commanders" series at the University of Oklahoma Press. Among his many much-respected works on military history, he has published *Custer Victorious: The Civil War Battles of General George Armstrong Custer* (Fairleigh Dickinson University Press, 1983), and, as editor, *Black Flag over Dixie: Racial Atrocities and Reprisals in the Civil War* (Southern Illinois University Press, 2004).

Index

Anita Palladino, ed., *Diary of a Yankee Engineer: The Civil War Story of John H. Westervelt, Engineer, 1st New York Volunteer Engineer Corps.*

Herman Belz, *Abraham Lincoln, Constitutionalism, and Equal Rights in the Civil War Era.*

Earl J. Hess, *Liberty, Virtue, and Progress: Northerners and Their War for the Union.* Second revised edition, with a new introduction by the author.

William L. Burton, *Melting Pot Soldiers: The Union's Ethnic Regiments.*

Hans L. Trefousse, *Carl Schurz: A Biography.*

Stephen W. Sears, ed., *Mr. Dunn Browne's Experiences in the Army: The Civil War Letters of Samuel W. Fiske.*

Jean H. Baker, *Affairs of Party: The Political Culture of Northern Democrats in the Mid–Nineteenth Century.*

Frank L. Klement, *The Limits of Dissent: Clement L. Vallandigham and the Civil War.* With a new introduction by Steven K. Rogstad.

Lawrence N. Powell, *New Masters: Northern Planters during the Civil War and Reconstruction.*

John A. Carpenter, *Sword and Olive Branch: Oliver Otis Howard.*

Thomas F. Schwartz, ed., *"For a Vast Future Also": Essays from the* Journal of the Abraham Lincoln Association.

Mark De Wolfe Howe, ed., *Touched with Fire: Civil War Letters and Diary of Oliver Wendell Holmes, Jr.* With a new introduction by David Burton.

Harold Adams Small, ed., *The Road to Richmond: The Civil War Letters of Major Abner R. Small of the 16th Maine Volunteers.* With a new introduction by Earl J. Hess.

Eric A. Campbell, ed., *"A Grand Terrible Dramma": From Gettysburg to Petersburg: The Civil War Letters of Charles Wellington Reed.* Illustrated by Reed's Civil War sketches.

Herbert Mitgang, ed., *Abraham Lincoln: A Press Portrait.*

Harold Holzer, ed., *Prang's Civil War Pictures: The Complete Battle Chromos of Louis Prang.*

Harold Holzer, ed., *State of the Union: New York and the Civil War.*

Paul A. Cimbala and Randall M. Miller, eds., *Union Soldiers and the Northern Home Front: Wartime Experiences, Postwar Adjustments.*

Mark A. Snell, *From First to Last: The Life of Major General William B. Franklin.*

Paul A. Cimbala and Randall M. Miller, eds., *An Uncommon Time: The Civil War and the Northern Home Front.*

John Y. Simon and Harold Holzer, eds., *The Lincoln Forum: Rediscovering Abraham Lincoln.*

Thomas F. Curran, *Soldiers of Peace: Civil War Pacifism and the Postwar Radical Peace Movement.*

Kyle S. Sinisi, *Sacred Debts: State Civil War Claims and American Federalism, 1861–1880.*

Russell L. Johnson, *Warriors into Workers: The Civil War and the Formation of Urban-Industrial Society in a Northern City.*

Peter J. Parish, *The North and the Nation in the Era of the Civil War.* Edited by Adam L. P. Smith and Susan-Mary Grant.

Patricia Richard, *Busy Hands: Images of the Family in the Northern Civil War Effort.*

Michael S. Green, *Freedom, Union, and Power: The Mind of the Republican Party During the Civil War.*

Christian G. Samito, ed., *Fear Was Not In Him: The Civil War Letters of Major General Francis S. Barlow, U.S.A.*

John S. Collier and Bonnie B. Collier, eds., *Yours for the Union: The Civil War Letters of John W. Chase, First Massachusetts Light Artillery.*

Grace Palladino, *Another Civil War: Labor, Capital, and the State in the Anthracite Regions of Pennsylvania, 1840–1868.*

Christian B. Keller, *Chancellorsville and the Germans: Nativism, Ethnicity, and Civil War Memory.*

Robert M. Sandow, *Deserter Country: Civil War Opposition in the Pennsylvania Appalachians.*

Craig L. Symonds, ed., *Union Combined Operations in the Civil War.*

Harold Holzer, Craig L. Symonds, and Frank L. Williams, eds., *The Lincoln Assassination: Crime and Punishment, Myth and Memory.* A Lincoln Forum Book.

Earl F. Mulderink III, *New Bedford's Civil War.*

George Washington Williams, *A History of the Negro Troops in the War of the Rebellion, 1861–1865.* Introduction by John David Smith.

Randall M. Miller, ed., *Lincoln and Leadership: Military, Political, and Religious Decision Making.*

David G. Smith, *On the Edge of Freedom: The Fugitive Slave Issue in South Central Pennsylvania, 1820–1870.*

CPSIA information can be obtained at www.ICGtesting.com
Printed in the USA
LVOW131442040313

322623LV00001B/5/P